POCKE

TRACKS &
TRACKING
IN SOUTHERN AFRICA

LOUIS LIEBENBERG

Published by Struik Nature
(an imprint of Penguin Random House South Africa (Pty) Ltd)
Reg. No. 1953/000441/07
The Estuaries No. 4, Oxbow Crescent
Century Avenue, Century City, 7441
PO Box 1144, Cape Town, 8000 South Africa

Visit **www.struiknature.co.za** and join the Struik Nature
Club for updates, news, events and special offers.

For more information about tracking visit **www.cybertracker.org**

First published as *Photographic Guide to Tracks and Tracking in Southern Africa* in 2000
This reworked edition (*Pocket Guide Tracks & Tracking in Southern Africa*)
published in 2023

1 3 5 7 9 10 8 6 4 2

Publisher: Pippa Parker
Managing editor: Roelien Theron
Designer: Emily Vosloo
Typesetter: Deirdre Geldenhuys

Reproduction by Studio Repro
Printed and bound in China by Toppan Leefung
Packaging and Printing (Dongguan) Co., Ltd.

ISBN 9781775848714 (PRINT)
ISBN 9781775848721 (ePUB)

Front cover Cheetah, Namibia **Title page** Black-backed jackal, Botswana
Contents page Aardvark, Botswana **Back cover** (left to right) Péringuey's
adder and tracks; yellowbilled hornbill; lion spoor; hook-lipped rhinoceros

CONTENTS

INTRODUCTION: THE ART OF TRACKING

Tracking may well be among the oldest of the sciences. It is also one of the most revealing: trackers gain a detailed understanding of animal behaviour through the interpretation of their tracks and signs, gathering information – especially on seldom-seen rare or nocturnal species – which might otherwise remain unknown.

Moreover, tracks and signs illuminate natural behaviour, while direct observation often influences the animal by the mere presence of the observer. Tracking is thus a less invasive process than visual study, a method of information gathering in which the amount of stress inflicted on an animal is minimized.

One of the most important aids to successful nature conservation is, undoubtedly, an awareness of wildlife among the general public. Even keen nature lovers are often oblivious to the wealth of animal life around them, simply because most animals are rarely seen. Indeed, ignorance may well be the single most dangerous threat to species survival posed by human 'progress'. The ability to recognize living forms from the signs they leave helps create that awareness.

To the untrained eye the wilderness can appear desolate, but to someone who is 'spoor conscious' it will be full of life. Even if you never actually catch sight of the animals, you know that they are there, and by reconstructing their movements from the signs they leave behind, you will be able to visualize them, 'see' them in your mind's eye. In this way a whole story will unfold – a story of what happened when no-one was looking.

An African landscape, seemingly empty, but rich in wildlife

USING THIS BOOK

The species accounts in these pages are arranged in logical order, from reptiles and amphibians through the ground-feeding birds to the mammalian predators and herbivores. Each account carries at least one full-colour photograph of the relevant life form, illustrations of the footprint and, where appropriate, of other signs, and a brief description of the animal, its size, habitat, habits, food, spoor and other signs of its presence. The measurements given are those which the author has personally recorded. In some instances, further research is needed before the correct median – the average – can be firmly established.

The overall coverage is selective rather than comprehensive: the more common birds and reptiles (snakes appear in a composite entry) and most, though not all, the mammals are included. Of special interest is the feature (pages 14 and 15) on the tracks and signs of some of the more common insects one finds in veld and garden, and, on pages 136 and 137, a 'gallery' of pictures comprising a representative selection of animal droppings. Distribution maps have been included where appropriate. Also included are a glossary and an index.

TRACKS AND SIGNS

Tracking involves each and every indication of an animal's presence, including ground spoor, vegetation spoor, scent, feeding signs, urine, faeces, saliva, pellets, territorial signs, paths and shelters, vocal and other auditory signs, visual signs, incidental signs, circumstantial signs and skeletal signs.

Footprints provide the most detailed information on the identity, movements and activities of animals in the wild. The spoor illustrations presented in this book derive from precise studies that were made under ideal conditions.

In reality, though, one seldom finds two animals of the same species with identical footprints: nature simply does not work in that way. But these 'ideal' footprints do provide images that improve one's chances of recognizing spoor that may otherwise be overlooked. Conversely, the preconceived images could prompt 'recognition' of patterns in markings made by other animals, or even random markings, so one must always be careful not to see simply what one wants to see.

While species may be recognized by general characteristics, each individual animal's spoor has its subtle distinctions. These differences are dictated by age, mass, sex, physical condition, the local terrain and the broader region (the nature of which gives rise to functional and environmental adaptations). The animal may also have a unique way of walking or a particular habit that distinguishes it from others. And, of course, there are random variations.

Thus, for example, the San trackers of the Kalahari, whose skill has been honed over many generations, can follow a particular antelope, perhaps one they have wounded, and distinguish it from the rest of the herd. They are also able to track fellow humans, identifying not only the gender but the particular individual they are tracking. Women usually have smaller and narrower, and sometimes more 'curvaceous', feet than men; a slender body build usually means slender feet; stocky people tend to have shorter and broader feet. A person's spoor is characterized by the way he or she treads and walks, by the length of stride, the way the ball of the foot is twisted, the way the toes point and whether they are splayed or curled in, by the way the foot throws up small sprays of sand, and by the scuff marks. Each person covers the ground in unique fashion.

The San are master trackers; this tracker is !Nate of Lone Tree, Botswana.

Many animals in the wild are not so individualized. While the spoor of most of the larger mammals and birds will reveal the particular species to which they belong, those of the smaller animals may indicate only the broader genus, family or order. The smaller the animal, in short, the more difficult it becomes to pinpoint its precise classification.

The clearest footprints tend to be left in damp, slightly muddy earth, in wet sand, in a thin layer of loose dust on firm substrate (a dirt road or path, for example), and in snow. Usually, however, footprints are partially obliterated, and one should explore the area – walk up and down the trail – to find the best imprints. Even if no clear prints are discerned, the information from a number of footprints can be pieced together to produce a composite image of the complete spoor.

Soft sand is always a difficult spoor medium. Try to visualize the shape of the footprint before the loose grains rolled together and blurred the edges. Bear in mind, too, that slipping and twisting will distort footprints in any kind of terrain: when the animal runs, or walks on a slope, its feet may slide and spoor will appear elongated or warped. Moreover, when the animal trots or runs, its mass is supported largely by the toes and only part of the intermediate pads may show (in the case of mongooses, the proximal pads may not show at all). Similarly, hard ground may only reveal claw marks.

When confronted by a choice of several possible species, consult the distribution maps in this book, eliminating those that do not occur in the area. Then narrow the list down by noting any feeding signs, faeces, and such elements of habit and habitat as daily rhythm and sociability.

Spoor identification requires field skill as well as knowledge. Although the novice naturalist should be able to use this book to identify near-perfect spoor in ideal conditions, it is only by accumulating experience that one learns to interpret imperfect signs, especially those imprinted in loose sand. Practice, as always, is the key to success.

LEARNING TO TRACK

Those who are not traditional hunters cannot really expect to reach the same level of skill as folk for whom tracking becomes part of their way of life in childhood, and whose very survival depends on their tracking abilities. This book, however, will introduce readers to the basics, help them identify species from the signs the animals leave behind. The average person should, with regular practice, be able to become a fair tracker. Among the qualities required are good eyesight (or good glasses), acute observation, a degree of physical fitness, patience, perseverance, concentration, imagination and a good memory.

The ease or difficulty of tracking at any given time also depends on a number of other factors. The type of ground and vegetation and weather conditions will determine the degree of skill needed to recognize and interpret spoor. It is more difficult, for example, to track in hard, stony terrain than in firm sand. Spoor lacks depth in overcast weather, while it may be obliterated entirely by rain. In areas of high animal densities the spoor may be blurred or otherwise confused.

The easiest way to learn the art of tracking is to have an experienced tracker teach you, to point out and explain all the signs until you are able to recognize and interpret them yourself. Bear in mind, though, that expert trackers are few and far between and many are unfamiliar with the English language.

Red lechwe track on firm substrate

A valid option is to teach yourself. This approach is much more time-consuming, of course, but it has its rewards, most notably the excitement and the sense of achievement that comes with making one's own discoveries.

Start by studying your own tracks. Adopt an initial two-phase approach, repeating the phases until they come together to become one sequence, as follows.

Phase One. Mark the starting point, and then lay out a spoor for yourself. Go back to the start, and study every sign of your passage. When you complete the course – which may take some while – return to the starting point.

Phase Two. The course now consists of two trails, and since you've been over it twice, you should know where it is going. This second phase involves simply walking over a familiar course at fast pace. Look well ahead of you, try to pick up as many signs in the wider area as possible. The objective is to develop the ability to anticipate and predict the unfamiliar.

In Phase One you focus on recognition and interpretation and ignore such aspects as momentum and anticipation. By Phase Two you are familiar with the spoor and should now concentrate on these aspects. You'll probably miss most of the signs on the first Phase Two run, but will recognize more of them, and more quickly, after going over the ground several times. The combined exercise should be repeated over different types of terrain, starting with an easy route, perhaps over softish sand, and gradually working up towards the more difficult types.

When you have developed an ability to track your own trail, get someone else to lay one down for you. This spoor will of course be more difficult. Obviously it is easier if you use a person rather than an animal as your quarry at this stage, since you can identify with another human being, and anticipate their movements by putting yourself in their position.

Phases One and Two involved the location and observation of each and every sign. In the third exercise, try to follow the trail by looking at only a few signs. Survey the terrain; try to imagine the most likely route the person would have taken; try to spot signs well ahead, neglecting those in between. Short cuts will save a lot of time and trouble. Indeed, if you know the area and the person well and can calculate his or her route through a certain point, skip the intermediate signs, go straight to that point and track the trail from there. If you lose the spoor, search other possible routes for signs. Should this prove unsuccessful, walk in a series of ever-widening circles in order to find fresh leads.

So much for the human trail: tracking wildlife poses much more of a challenge. Here, the best way to start is to watch the animal and, once it has moved off, approach and study its tracks. Follow the trail (you'll know the direction in which it moved); study the signs carefully so that you become familiar with

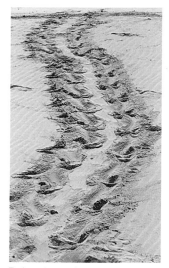

Turtle track on sand

the animal's habits, its footprints, its gait. Gradually upgrade the challenge. Begin with easy terrain, such as the sand of beach dunes or that of an arid region, progressing to terrain with soft substrate and sparse vegetation, then to soft substrate and denser vegetation, then to harder, stony ground with sparser cover, and finally to harder, stony substrate with dense vegetation. Eventually, as you build up experience, it will be possible to track an animal without observing all the signs: a skilled tracker will know the animal well enough to predict its movements.

Expert trackers will also need to know whether a spoor is fresh enough to follow up, or just too old to be worthwhile. Tracks of other animals that superimpose or underlie the spoor may help them to estimate its age. They will also need to tell when the spoor is so fresh, and the animal so close, that it will be alarmed if they do not approach it with stealth. Again, this requires knowledge of animal behaviour, a familiarity with local weather conditions, and a great deal of practice. The rate at and the way in which the sun, wind and rain erode the tracks can vary considerably.

Study the aging process systematically. Lay out a series of spoor – say, one footprint each hour – over a full day. By evening you will have examples of spoor of varying ages, they can be compared directly, and you will be able to study the aging process at your leisure and in detail. Repeat the exercise in different kinds of soil, on different types of terrain, in different seasons and in various weather conditions.

TRACKING IN NATURE CONSERVATION

Trackers play a key role in the growing ecotourism industry, serving as the eyes and ears of those who embark on game-viewing drives and wilderness trails.

They are also crucial in anti-poaching operations. Intruders may be detected even when they leave no clearly discernible human footprints. For example, fleeing animals will leave tracks that indicate a disturbance – a human-inspired one if there are no signs of a natural predator. Scavenger spoor converging on a point may also indicate the presence of a large carcass, perhaps of an animal killed by poachers.

Karel Benadie with the CyberTracker in the Karoo

Close-up of the CyberTracker: data at the touch of a button

Expert trackers, able to garner information denied to conventional observers, also render valuable assistance to researchers studying animal behaviour. Combining traditional tracking with modern technology, such as radio tracking, allows the researcher to accomplish much more than either method could on its own.

At the leading edge of the technology is the CyberTracker field computer, a device that enables trackers to record all their field observations, and to store them in a database for future reference. An integrated Global Positioning System (GPS) records the location, time and date of each entry by means of satellite navigation. The data collected can also be fed into a Geographic Information System (GIS). All of this may sound rather complex, but in fact the system is easy to use in terms of both input and access: managers and other interested parties are able to call up the maps, tables and other graphics to analyze data and to monitor long-term trends at the touch of a button.

READING THE SIGNS

Short of direct visual observation, an animal's track – its footprint – provides the surest clue to its presence (or passage) and its identity. However, animals can often be detected and sometimes identified by a variety of other signs, including scuff marks, broken twigs, freshly turned stones, leaves and other objects, trampled and horned vegetation, riverbank mud displacement, droppings, pellets and latrines.

Droppings

Faeces are among the more obvious of these supplementary signs. Those of elephants, rhinos and hippos, for example, are large and rounded; hippos tend to scatter theirs with a paddle-like action of their tails, often found on or near the paths along the riverbanks that serve as their night-time feeding grounds. Rhinos defecate in territorial middens. Zebra dung has a distinctive and regular kidney shape; warthog droppings are similar in appearance, but more irregular and rounder.

Antelope tend to have similar-shaped droppings – pellet-like, with a point at one end and an indentation at the other – so it can be hard to identify a particular species from this sign alone. Often, the best one can do is make a rough estimate of the animal's size (small, medium, large). Giraffe droppings are similar to the antelopes' but are larger and, because they fall from a height, tend to be scattered.

Most mammalian carnivores leave narrow, cylindrical or sausage-shaped droppings that are pointed at one end. Omnivores, such as baboons and honey badgers, also tend to produce cylindrical droppings, as do the plant-eating porcupines.

Droppings often reveal what an animal eats, which is a more than useful pointer to species identification. The dung of the hook-lipped (black) rhino, for example, contains the remains of twigs and leaves; the square-lipped (white) rhino's faeces reveal its grass diet. Carnivore faeces tend to show bone and hair; hyaenas, and sometimes lions, produce droppings that are whitish from the high calcium content of their bone diet. Conversely, a lion's faeces can often be black from the amount of blood it has consumed. Civet droppings are invariably characterized by a mixture of millipede shells, fruit pips, insect husks and fur and bone from the tiny mammals they prey on; those of otters and water mongooses by crabshells; aardvarks and aardwolfs

Springhare droppings: almost rectangular with one pointed end

by a mix of sand and termite remains; pangolins by sand and ant remains. Wetland trees are frequently stained white with the guano of roosting herons, egrets and cormorants; white-stained rocks can indicate the nesting site of a Cape vulture, bald ibis, marabou stork, black eagle or some other raptor. Dassies stain the rocky outcrops among which they live white and dark brown with their urine.

Territorial markings

Many animals use their faeces to mark out their territories, and you'll often come across their waste, in huge quantities, in areas called middens or latrines. The animal keeps returning to its latrine, and in doing so leaves other signs of its presence, such as scrapings and rubbing posts. The latter are smooth, well-worn rocks, trees, or stumps used for scraping off dead skin, parasites and other unwanted matter.

Other territorial markings include clawing posts; ground that has been pawed; shrubbery that has been horned; and twigs that have been covered in tarry secretions produced by antelope – such as dik-dik, red duiker and blue duiker – in the preorbital gland. Vegetation is covered by secretions from the anal gland in hyaenas, polecats, civets and others. Some mammals – rhino, lion and leopard, for instance – spray vegetation with their urine.

Feeding signs

Uprooted trees, scattered grass tufts, stripped bark and broken branches may indicate the presence of elephants, though not always. Porcupines ringbark trees, as do many other rodents; browsers leave jagged leaf edges; and hook-lipped (black) rhinos make neat, angular bite marks on twigs. Other browsers deposit saliva – copious amounts of it, dripping down in streams in the case of the giraffe, which eats the leaves and flowers of thorny acacias.

The general nature of cropped vegetation is usually a good pointer to the type of animal that has been browsing it. One can at least make a rough estimate of the animal's size from the level at which it eats. Grazers also feed at different levels, and on different lengths of grass: buffalo and zebra prefer the longer type, around which they can wrap their tongues, while wildebeest and square-lipped (white) rhino tend to crop close to the ground.

Among other useful feeding signs are carcasses and skeletons, which indicate recent activity and will convey some idea of the type of carnivore or scavenger that has been feeding. Generally speaking, the larger the carcass, the larger the predator. Beak and bite marks, and the part of the animal consumed, are significant pointers; so, too, is the position of the carcass: leopards, for instance, often carry their prey into a tree. Old rodent and other bones strewn beneath a tree will invariably pinpoint the location of a raptor's nest.

Carcasses provide good pointers to what killed the animals.

Birds, snakes and, often, hyaenas, regurgitate pellets of hair, shell, insect chitin, bones and other indigestible material. But look closely: the pellets can be confused with long, cylindrical dung, especially that of carnivores.

Other signs

Nests, depressions in vegetation and holes in trees or the ground also serve as useful aids to identification. Squirrel tracks, for instance, almost always lead to and from a tree, and keeping vigil over a tree hollow might well yield a sighting of squirrel, bushbaby or bird. Even more distinctive are birds' nests. The hamerkop's huge, dome-like structure is unmistakable; white-backed vultures make their acacia-based homes in untidy clusters of twigs; buffalo weavers construct untidy stick nests, a little way down from the top of particular trees; swallows and swifts build mud nests on buildings and cliff sides. Among the most eye-catching of all are the vast colonial nests fashioned by sociable weavers.

Then there's the all-purpose aardvark hole, originally excavated by this nocturnal insectivore and then given over to a whole succession of squatters. Many different species, including hyaena, warthog and mongoose, are known to use the aardvark's abandoned home. The tracks and droppings around the hole, and indeed its size, will give one a good idea of which particular animal is in residence.

WILDLIFE IN MINIATURE

Most terrestrial life forms leave signs of their presence in and passage through their home range – not least of all the arthropods, big and small, which inhabit our gardens and the countryside beyond. The tracks illustrated here (and best observed on smooth, sandy soil) are those of a few of our more familiar arthropods.

Caterpillar

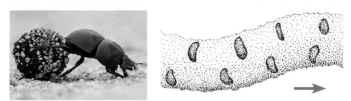

Millipede

Dung beetle

Termite

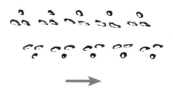

Grasshopper

Tenebrionid beetle

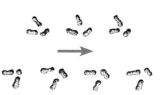

Scorpion

15

Frogs and Toads   Class Amphibia

Southern Africa is home to many species of frogs and toads, collectively known as Anura. They are, of course, excellent swimmers and, on land, adapted for a leaping mode of locomotion. **Size** Ranges from the 18mm microfrog to bullfrogs that grow to more than 200mm in length. **Habitat** Some frogs and toads are wholly aquatic; others semi-aquatic, inhabiting marshy ground near watercourses, vleis and dams. In general, toads prefer more open country and are generally less aquatic than frogs. **Habits** Most species are active at night, and at twilight and just before dawn. **Food** Insects, insect larvae and snails. **Spoor** Anura have four toes on each forefoot and five toes on each hind foot. The hopping spoor of a toad shows the five toes of the hind feet and the imprints of the four toes of the forefeet. **Other signs:** The droppings, especially those of toads, are short and compact and contain the remains of insect exoskeletons and snail shells.

A brightly coloured painted reed frog

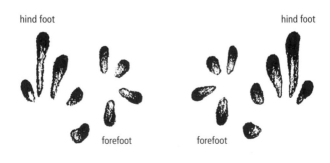

hind foot   hind foot

forefoot   forefoot

Land Tortoises   Family Testudinidae

These shell-backed and toothless reptiles are well represented in southern Africa, with 12 species found in the region. They are characterized by their dome-like shells and clawed feet. **Size** Ranges from the leopard tortoise (45cm) to the speckled padloper (9cm), the world's smallest. **Habitat** Tortoises cannot tolerate temperature extremes, and need good ground cover in which to shelter from both heat and cold. **Habits** For protection, the tortoise withdraws its head and limbs into its shell. Adult males are aggressive towards each other in the mating season. In very cold periods, tortoises find a sheltered place in which to hibernate. Tortoises lay eggs, which they bury in the ground to incubate. **Food** Mainly plant matter, though some species eat snails, millipedes and other invertebrates; others will gnaw bones and even eat carnivore droppings for the calcium. **Spoor** Two species, the greater padloper and the parrot-beaked tortoise, have four claws on the forefeet and hind feet. All other land tortoises, including three species of padlopers, have five claws on the forefeet and four on the hind feet. Claws may be dragged through soft sand; only the claw marks may show on hard ground. **Other signs:** Droppings, comprising mainly vegetable matter, resemble those of a small carnivore (cylindrical, and pointed at one end).

Angulate tortoise

forefoot

hind foot

17

Side-necked Terrapins   Family Pelomedusidae

Terrapins occur in fresh water and are characterized by their webbed toes. There are two distinct types within the region: the common marsh terrapin and the hinged terrapins, of which there are five species. **Size** Length 15–45cm. **Habitat** The helmeted terrapin is widespread, found wherever there are pans, lakes, rivers and swamps. They will also bask on logs, rocks and river banks. The hinged terrapins are confined to the northern areas. **Habits** Like tortoises, terrapins retreat into their shells for protection but do so by bending their necks sideways. **Food** Terrapins are carnivorous for the most part, feeding on fish and on birds that come to the water to drink. They have also been known to scavenge at hippo, crocodile and antelope carcasses, and to feed on hippo skin, which they nip off (very painfully) near the anal area. **Spoor** These terrapins have five claws on both the forefeet and hind feet.

Serrated hinged terrapins

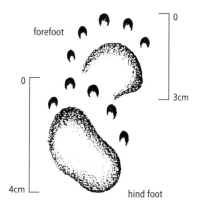

18

Sea Turtles   Superfamily Chelonioidea

Five species of these marine reptiles occur along southern Africa's coasts though only two, the giant leatherback and the loggerhead, venture ashore. Limbs have been modified into flippers, which retain just one or two claws. Unlike tortoises and terrapins, the turtle cannot withdraw into its shell (or carapace). **Size** Length 70–178cm. **Habitat** Leatherbacks and loggerheads arrive at their breeding grounds off southern Africa's eastern seaboard, from about Cape Vidal northwards, each year between November and January. **Habits** Mating takes place offshore. When the time is right, the females crawl up the beaches at night to lay and bury their eggs. **Food** Seaweed, seagrasses, jellyfish, combjellies, corals, sea urchins, giant clams, crustaceans (mostly shrimps, prawns and crabs) and fish. Not all turtles, however, are carnivorous; some species are restricted in their diet to seaweeds and seagrasses. **Spoor** Loggerheads and leatherbacks leave a distinct trail on the beach sand.

Loggerhead turtle

Loggerhead turtle eggs

Turtle tracks on a beach

Snakes   Suborder Serpentes

These limbless, scaly reptiles vary widely in size, colour, markings and habitat. **Size** From small up to 7m in length. **Habitat** Depends on the species, of which about 175 occur in southern Africa. Snakes are found in deserts and semi-arid areas, in forests, grasslands and even in the sea. All are cold-blooded, and are at their most active within their preferred temperature range of 20–32° Celsius. **Habits** When ambient temperature becomes too hot snakes move into shade; in cold conditions they become sluggish; in very cold ones they may hibernate. Vision is acute at short range and poor at a distance. They are highly sensitive to vibrations. **Food** Most snakes prefer live prey (small mammals, birds, other reptiles, amphibians, insects and other invertebrates), which is swallowed whole. **Spoor** Snakes use their bodies to move in either rectilinear (caterpillar-like) or undulatory fashion.

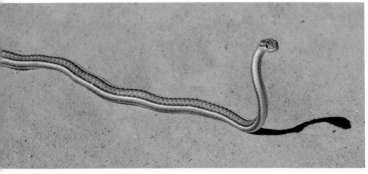

Fork-marked sand snake (*Psammophis trinasalis*)

Puff adder trail

Sand snake trail

Rectilinear progression – forward movement in a straight line – is characteristic of heavy-bodied snakes such as pythons and adders in leisurely mode. Here, the belly muscles move the large ventral plates (belly scales) forward in alternate waves to enable the overlapping plate-edges to get a grip on any rough features on the ground so that the body is drawn forward over them. With puff adders, there is usually a thin furrow down the middle of the trail where the snake has dragged the tip of its tail, and the ventral scales may leave clear markings. The spoor of puff adders and pythons can be distinguished by markings left by the ventral scales of each species: the middle row of the puff adder's spoor is almost as wide as the spoor itself; the python's is much narrower, so adjacent rows of scales also mark the spoor.

Undulatory or *serpentine progression* involves a series of sideways motions, 'rippling' from front to back, where each outward bend or curve of the snake's body pushes up against an uneven or rough surface and propels the snake forward. Most snakes cover the ground in this way – including pythons and puff adders when they are in a hurry (it is a much faster method). The sidewinding variation, in which the body is lifted from the ground in undulating motions, is characteristic of small, desert-living adders.

Other signs: Snakes moult periodically, and discarded skin may be found near their burrows.

The best time to follow snake spoor is in the early morning, before the wind obliterates the traces. To determine direction, study the way the sand or earth has been pushed back.

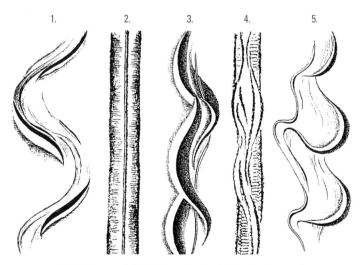

1. Typical snake   2. Puff adder (rectilinear)   3. Puff adder (undulatory)
4. Python (rectilinear)   5. Python (undulatory)

Rock Monitor *Varanus albigularis*

A very large, stout lizard with strong, stocky limbs and sharp claws. The back is dark grey-brown with pale yellow, dark-edged blotches; limbs are spotted with pale yellow; the tail is banded in dark brown and off-white. **Size** Length 70–110cm. **Habitat** Savanna and arid, karroid areas. **Habits** Usually solitary; takes shelter in trees, often under loose bark. **Food** Mainly invertebrates (millipedes, beetles, grasshoppers and land snails). Also scavenges on carrion. **Spoor** Monitors have five toes on each fore- and hind foot; each toe has a strong, sharp claw. In muddy terrain, the scales underneath the toes show clearly in the spoor. The tail also leaves a clear drag mark.

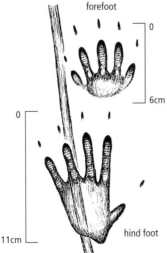

forefoot

0

6cm

0

11cm

hind foot

22

Water Monitor *Varanus niloticus*

This reptile, the largest of the African lizards, has a stout body, powerful limbs and strong claws. It is greyish brown to dirty olive-brown on the top of its head and back, with scattered darker blotches and light yellow ocelli and bands on the head, back and limbs. Belly and throat are paler, with black bars. **Size** Length 1–1.4m. **Habitat** Rivers, pans and major lakes; always found in the vicinity of permanent water. **Habits** An excellent swimmer. **Food** Forages in freshwater pools for crabs and mussels, frogs, fish, birds and their eggs. **Spoor** Like that of the rock monitor (see opposite), this species' spoor shows five toes on the fore- and hind feet. The tail leaves a clear drag mark.

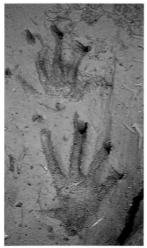

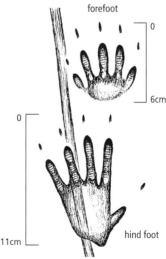

forefoot

0

6cm

0

11cm

hind foot

Nile Crocodile *Crocodylus niloticus*

The largest of Africa's reptiles, occasionally reaching a mass of more than 1 000kg. The nostril, eye and ear openings are located at the top of the head, projecting just above the surface when the animal is floating. **Size** Length 2.5–3.5m, max. 5.9m. **Habitat** Large rivers, lakes and swamps; river mouths, estuaries and mangrove swamps. **Habits** Amphibious and riparian (river environment). Spends much of the day basking in the sun, on sand- or mudbanks, in order to gain heat; the rest of the time it remains semi-submerged. **Food** Subadults feed on fish, insects, frogs, terrapins, birds and small mammals; adults mainly on fish, and on mammals as substantial as medium to large antelope, zebra and even buffalo, which are ambushed when they come to the water to drink. **Spoor** Crocodiles have five toes on the forefeet and four on the hind feet. Each toe has a thick claw. The hind feet are webbed. In mud, the scales underneath the feet leave clear impressions in the spoor. The drag mark of the tail shows in the trail. The tracks of a young crocodile can be distinguished from that of monitors by the four hind toes (monitors have five). **Other signs:** These include the croaks of the young crocodiles while hatching and when they are in the nursery area. The remains of the large, white eggs, usually left on sandy patches, show where a crocodile has been breeding.

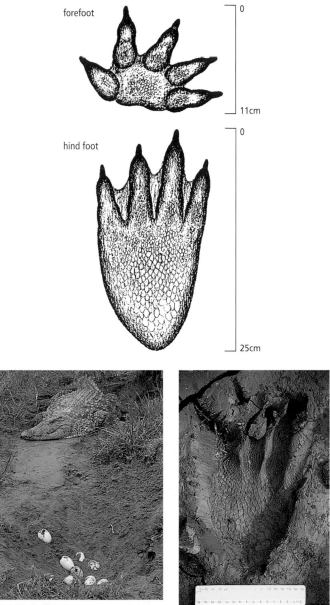

forefoot

0

11cm

hind foot

0

25cm

Nest of crocodile eggs

25

Passerines   Order Passeriformes

The order is represented by more than 5 000 small to large species worldwide, among them crows, ravens, sparrows, waxbills, canaries, buntings, wagtails, starlings, bulbuls, thrushes, chats and larks. They are represented in southern Africa by 43 families, most of which (about 80 per cent) are arboreal. Size, habits and feeding patterns vary widely. **Spoor** Three toes in front, one behind, which is adapted for perching. No species has webbed toes. Passerine spoor will often superimpose or underlie, and therefore help to age, larger animal tracks.

Cape sparrow

Crows and Ravens   Family Corvidae

Large, predominantly black birds with slender bills and large, strong feet. **Size** 43–54cm. **Habitat** Wide tolerance. **Habits** Usually seen in pairs, sometimes in flocks. These birds forage on the ground, walking with long strides. **Food** Omnivorous. **Spoor** All have three forward-pointing toes and one pointing back at an angle.

Black crow

Hornbills   Family Bucerotidae

In southern Africa these would include the yellowbilled, redbilled and grey hornbills, all medium-sized birds with large, heavy, deeply curved bills. Another member, the distinctive southern ground hornbill is treated separately (see page 28). Most are black, grey and white in colour with broad wings and long tails. **Size** 42–60cm. **Habitat** Mainly forest, woodland and bushveld. **Habits** Found singly or in pairs or small groups; forages mostly on the ground but also in trees. **Food** Insects. **Spoor** Legs are very short (unlike those of the southern ground hornbill) and stout. Toes short, the third and fourth joined at the base; claws short, curved and with sharp edges. All have similar spoor, with three forward-pointing toes and one backward-pointing toe.

Yellowbilled hornbill

Redbilled hornbill

0

6cm

Southern Ground Hornbill *Bucorvus leadbeateri*

A very large turkey-like bird, mostly black with distinctive red wattles. **Size** 90–129cm. **Habitat** Woodland, savanna, open grassveld and agricultural land. **Habits** Forages on the ground; found in pairs or groups of, usually, not more than eight. **Food** The ground hornbill is wholly carnivorous, its diet including reptiles, frogs, snails and insects. **Spoor** The legs are long, and the toes short, with the third and fourth joined at the base. Claws are short, curved and with sharp edges.

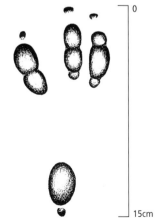

0

15cm

Doves and Pigeons   Family Columbidae

Medium-sized birds with short bills. **Size** 19–36cm. **Habitat** Found everywhere: woodland, forest, savanna, grassland, riverine bush, farmland, urban and rural gardens and city parks. **Habits** Solitary or found in pairs or flocks. **Food** Seeds, insects, fallen grain, winged termites and fruits. **Spoor** These birds forage on the ground, walking with small steps in 'pigeon-toed' fashion to leave a winding trail. The different species have similar tracks, comprising three forward-pointing toes and an angled backward-pointing toe. Dove footprints are smaller than those of pigeons. The Namaqua dove, smallest of the region's doves, has a dragging spoor.

Cape turtle dove

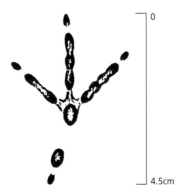

Crowned Lapwing Vanellus coronatus

A fairly large plover with long, red legs. The face, chest and upper parts are greyish brown, the crown is black, ringed with white. A dark breastband separates the brown chest from a white belly. **Size** 30cm. **Habitat** Short, dry grassland, burnt veld, lightly wooded savanna and semidesert. **Habits** Gregarious, often active and vocal at night. **Food** Insects. **Spoor** Tracks show three forward-pointing toes (no back toe).

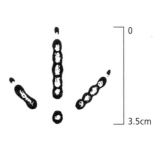

Blacksmith Lapwing Vanellus armatus

A medium-sized, boldly coloured, black, white and grey lapwing. The back and wings are greyish and the underparts black from chin to upper belly. **Size** 30cm. **Habitat** Shorelines of dams, pans, vleis and sewage ponds; also short grassy verges of inland waters, large lawns and playing fields. **Habits** Often solitary or in pairs. Silent when foraging or resting, usually calling in flight when alarmed. **Food** Insects, worms and molluscs. **Spoor** Three widely splayed, thin toes; hind toe absent.

Spotted Thick-knee *Burhinus capensis*

A medium-sized bird, spotted dark brown or buff above, white below, with large, yellow eyes, and yellow legs and feet. **Size** 42–44cm. **Habitat** Open grassland, savanna, stony semidesert with scrub, wide marine beaches; also agricultural land. **Habits** Found singly or in pairs; nocturnal and crepuscular. **Food** Insects, crustaceans, molluscs, frogs and grass seeds. **Spoor** The toes are short, and slightly webbed at the base. The hind toe is absent.

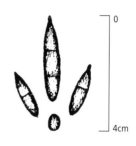

Francolins Family Phasianidae

Cryptically coloured terrestrial or ground-living game birds. **Size** 28–42cm. **Habitat** Bushveld, grass and thickets at edges of woodland; cultivated lands, savanna, riverine bush and vleis. **Habits** Found singly, in pairs or in coveys of up to eight birds. Roosts in trees or on the ground at night. **Food** Seeds, berries, roots, bulbs, insects and snails. **Spoor** Three forward-pointing toes with an angled backward-pointing toe. **Other signs:** Loud alarm call.

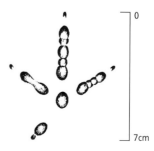

Swainson's francolin

Guineafowl Family Numididae

There are two species in this family in southern Africa.
Size 50–58cm. **Habitat** Helmeted guineafowl: open
grassland, vleis, savanna, cultivated lands, edge of Karoo
scrub and bushveld. Crested guineafowl: montane, riparian,
dune and coastal forests. **Habits** Gregarious. **Food** Seeds,
bulbs, tubers, berries, insects, snails, ticks, millipedes and fallen grain. **Spoor**
Three forward-pointing toes and one angled backward-pointing toe.

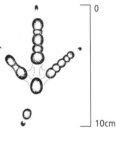

Helmeted guineafowl   Crested guineafowl

Korhaans *Eupodotis* species

Medium-sized birds with yellow legs, robust bodies, long necks and large
heads. **Size** Length 50–53cm; mass 670–715g. **Habitat** Widespread. **Habits**
Usually solitary, sometimes found in pairs. **Food** Mainly plant material; also
insects. **Spoor** Short, thick toes; the hind toe is absent.

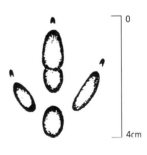

Red-crested korhaan

Kori Bustard   *Ardeotis kori*

Said to be the heaviest of all flying birds; greyish brown above, with a white belly, neck and a breast which is finely barred (though it looks grey from a distance). The head is slightly crested with a longish bill. **Size** 1.2–1.5m.

Habitat Open plains of the Karoo, highveld grassland, Kalahari sandveld, arid scrub, Namib Desert, lightly wooded savanna and bushveld. **Habits** Solitary or in pairs when breeding, otherwise gregarious, gathering in flocks of up to 40 or more individuals. **Food** Insects, small vertebrates, carrion, seeds and gum. **Spoor** Long legs with short, thick toes; the hind toe is absent.

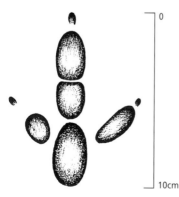

Blue Crane   *Grus paradisea*

This beautiful bird is uniformly blue-grey, with long slate-grey tail feathers curving to the ground. **Size** 1.02–1.07m. **Habitat** Midland and highland grassveld, fringes of Karoo, cultivated land and edges of vleis. **Habits** Highly gregarious when not breeding, otherwise found in pairs or family groups. **Food** Frogs, reptiles, insects, fish, grain, green shoots and grass seeds. **Spoor** Long legs, but short toes; the hind toe is reduced and elevated.

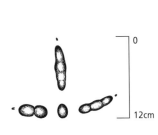

0

12cm

Red-knobbed Coot   *Fulica cristata*

A medium-sized bird, black with white bill and frontal shield backed by two dark red knobs. **Size** 43cm. **Habitat** Inland waters. **Habits** Spends most of its time in open water. **Food** Water plants, grass, insects and seeds. **Spoor** A distinctive track, created by the scalloped webbing on the toes. The hind toe is angled slightly. **Other signs:** Very large mound-like nests of aquatic vegetation. Eggs are laid on top.

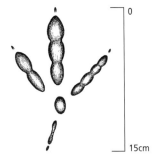

0

15cm

Ostrich *Struthio camelus*

The world's largest living bird. Males are black with white wings, females brownish grey. **Size** Up to 2m in height. **Habitat** Bushveld to desert. **Habits** Found in flocks of 30–40 birds when not breeding. **Food** Grass, berries, seeds, succulent plants, small reptiles and insects. **Spoor** Legs are very long with only two toes. **Other signs:** The eggs are unmistakable, large and laid in communal, earthen nests which will be defended by a single male. Ostriches also produce copious amounts of mixed liquid and solid waste. Like that of all birds, their urea stains the droppings white. The call is a deep boom, not unlike the roar of a lion (for which it is often mistaken). Incidental signs include large discarded feathers.

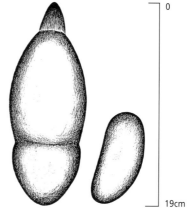

0

19cm

Secretarybird   *Sagittarius serpentarius*

A very large bird with long legs and tail. The body is mainly pale grey, with black belly, leg feathering, rump and crest feathers. The long crest is erectile. **Size** 1.25–1.5m in height. **Habitat** Semidesert, grassland, savanna, open woodland, farmland and mountain slopes. **Habits** Usually found in pairs, sometimes in groups of three or four. **Food** Insects, rodents, frogs, toads, lizards and snakes, young hares and the young and eggs of various other birds. **Spoor** Short toes webbed at the base, with strong claws. **Other signs:** The bird builds a large flat platform of sticks in the tops of dense thorntrees.

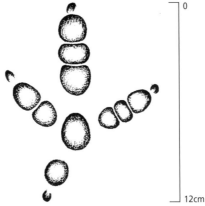

Vultures   Family Accipitridae

Southern Africa is home to nine species of these large, scavenging birds. They have very broad wings, enabling them to ride the thermals. Eyesight is highly developed; the head is usually naked of feathers to prevent fouling while feeding. **Size** 64–120cm. **Habitat** Widely distributed across the northern parts of the subcontinent; the Cape vulture's range extends to the southern coast. **Habits** Most visible when they soar above the plains in search of carrion, coming together in a feeding frenzy when a carcass is spotted. **Food** Carrion and bone fragments. **Spoor** All vultures leave similar spoor, though track sizes differ according to species. Tracks are most easily seen around a carcass. **Other signs:** Nests are usually built, of twigs and branches, on the tops of trees; Cape and bearded vultures nest on cliff ledges.

Cape vulture

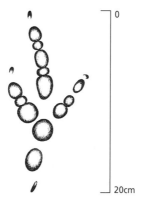

0

20cm

37

Herons   Family Ardeidae

Fairly large birds with slender necks and sharp beaks.
Size 97–140cm. **Habitat** Open grassland, the edges of
inland waters and forest clearings. **Habits** Herons wade in
shallows to feed; solitary when feeding. **Food** Frogs, fish,
crabs, insects, worms, rodents, small birds and reptiles.
Spoor Three forward-pointing toes and a back toe slightly off-centre.

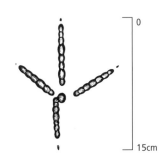

Grey heron

African Sacred Ibis   *Threskiornis aethiopicus*

One of four ibis species found in southern Africa, all with
identical spoor. The sacred ibis is mainly white with a black
head and neck. **Size** About 90cm. **Habitat** Varied; found in
coastal lagoons, tidal flats, offshore islands; also inland
downs. **Habits** Forages and scavenges. **Food** Insects, small
mammals and birds, eggs, reptiles, carrion and seeds. **Spoor** Legs are long,
with toes partly webbed at base. Three toes point forward; backward-pointing
toe at a slight angle.

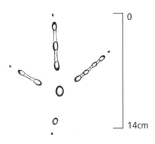

Egyptian Goose   *Alopochen aegyptiacus*

A large waterbird, brown above, greyish below, with dark-brown patches around the eyes and on the centre of the breast, and a dark brown collar on the neck. In flight the wings are white with black primaries and a green trailing edge. **Size** 63–73cm. **Habitat** Most inland waters – rivers, dams, floodplains, pans and marshes; also estuaries, coastal lakes and cultivated fields. **Habits** Highly gregarious. Young chicks will follow their mothers everywhere, and have been known to jump and 'parachute' down from great heights – from the trees or the buildings where they have built nests, for example, to be with her. **Food** Grass and leaves, seeds, grain, crop seedlings, aquatic rhizomes and tubers. **Spoor** The front toes of the bird are webbed; hind toes reduced.

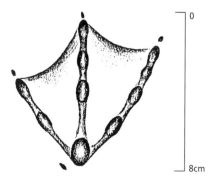

0

8cm

39

Rats and Mice   Families Cricetidae and Muridae

These rodents vary considerably in habits and habitat. Most of them are terrestrial, others burrow; most are nocturnal, although a few, like the four-striped grass mouse, are active during the day. **Size** From about 10cm head-to-tail up to the Gambian giant pouched rat's 80cm. **Habitat** Varied; nests may be in underground burrows, piles of vegetation, rock crevices or holes in tree trunks. **Habits** There are both solitary and gregarious forms. **Food** A variety of plant material, invertebrates, small snakes and lizards, birds' eggs and nestlings. **Spoor** Four toes show in the fore footprints, five toes in the hind footprints. When jumping, the hind prints appear ahead of the foreprints (see illustration, below).

Four-striped grass mouse

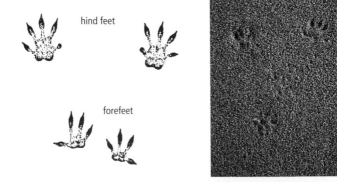

hind feet

forefeet

Example of the jumping spoor

Southern African Ground Squirrel   *Xerus inauris*

The upper parts of this rodent are cinnamon in colour, but individuals vary in shade. The belly is usually tinged buff. Lateral stripes run along either side of the body. **Size** Height 24cm; tail 21cm; mass 600g. **Habitat** Throughout the more arid parts of the subregion; the animal has a preference for open terrain with sparse bush cover. **Habits** Diurnal and terrestrial; gregarious; colonies of up to about 30 live in warrens with many entrances. **Food** Mainly vegetarian; diet includes leaves and stems of grasses, seeds, bulbs, roots and plant stems; some insect food. **Spoor** The ground squirrel has five toes on the forefoot, the first of which is rudimentary and without a claw; the hind foot also has five toes. Claws are long (about 10mm), sharp, slightly curved.

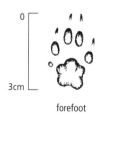

forefoot

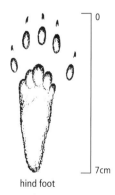

hind foot

Tree Squirrel *Paraxerus cepapi*

The species varies greatly in size and colour; pale grey overall in the western parts of its range, and darker, more buffy, sometimes rusty in the eastern parts. **Size** Height 18cm; tail 17cm; mass 200g. **Habitat** Savanna woodland of various types. **Habits** Generally solitary, but also occurs in pairs or in groups comprising a female with two or three young. The animal is both arboreal and terrestrial. **Food** Predominantly vegetarian; diet includes flowers, leaves, seeds, berries, fruits and bark; also insects. Feeding sites are marked by accumulations of the discarded (inedible) remains of the meal. **Spoor** The tree squirrel has four toes on the forefeet and five on the hind, each with short, sharp, curved claws adapted for arboreal life. The animal's trail nearly always starts and ends at the base of a tree; clawmarks can also be seen on the tree's bark.

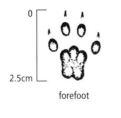

forefoot

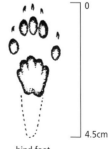

hind foot

Southern African Springhare   *Pedetes capensis*

With its short front legs, long powerful hind legs and long tail, the springhare bears a striking resemblance to a miniature kangaroo. **Size** Height 39cm; tail 40cm; mass 3.1kg. **Habitat** Widespread. **Habits** Nocturnal; congregates in scattered groups when feeding, usually within 250m of their burrows. **Food** Mainly grass. **Spoor** Five toes on the forefoot, with sharp, narrow, curved claws 18–20mm in length over the curve. Five toes on the hind feet, the first absent from the spoor, the second, third and fourth elongated (the third is the longest). The fifth claw (the shortest) does not mark in the spoor except when the animal sits up, in which case the whole hind foot, right back to the ankle, may show in the spoor. The marks of the front claws, used in excavation, can often be seen on the sides of a burrow, but seldom show in the spoor since the springhare usually moves on the hind feet – that is, it hops, holding the forelegs close to the body.

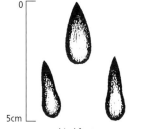

hind foot

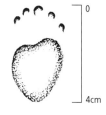

forefoot

Cape Porcupine   *Hystrix africaeaustralis*

The largest African rodent, characterized by its armoury of erectile spines and quills. **Size** Length 84cm; mass 18kg. **Habitat** Occurs in most types of vegetation. Shelters often contain accumulations of bones (a source of phosphate). **Habits** Almost exclusively nocturnal; usually solitary, occasionally found in pairs or in groups comprising female and young. Defends itself by rattling its quills to intimidate its attacker; also reverses into the intruder to dislodge barbed quills in its flesh. **Food** Predominantly vegetarian; diet includes bulbs, tubers, roots and fallen wild fruits; also gnaws the bark of trees. **Spoor** The porcupine has five toes on the front foot, the first toe reduced to a small stump without a claw. The other toes on the front feet have well-developed claws. Five toes on the hind foot, each with a claw. The fore- and hind feet each show three intermediate pads and two proximal pads in the spoor. The spoor also shows the marks of the quills, which are dragged. **Other signs:** One or more discarded quills.

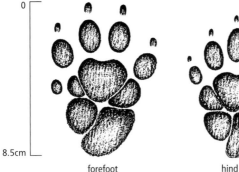

forefoot

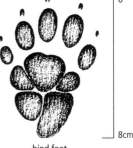

hind foot

Southern African Hedgehog   *Atelerix frontalis*

A small, spiny insectivore. **Size** 20cm in length; mass 400g. **Habitat** A wide variety of habitats, including scrub bush and grassland. **Habits** Predominantly nocturnal; rests by day curled up in debris in the shade of bushes, grass or holes. Has an acute sense of smell, but eyesight is poor. Usually slow in its movements; defends itself by rolling up into a ball; alarm call a high-pitched scream. **Food** Beetles, termites, centipedes, millipedes, grasshoppers, moths, earthworms, small mice, lizards, frogs, slugs, eggs and the chicks of terrestrial birds; also vegetable matter. **Spoor** The hedgehog has five toes on the front foot, the first of which shows behind the intermediate pad in the spoor; the hind foot has four toes, which are often dragged, leaving characteristic drag marks in the sand.

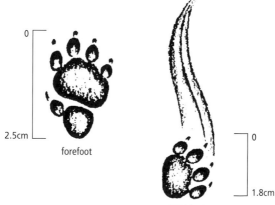

forefoot

hind foot

Hares   Family Leporidae

Southern Africa supports two species: the scrub hare *Lepus saxatilis*, and the Cape hare *Lepus capensis*. The former has grizzled greyish or buffy upperparts, while the Cape hare is light buff in colour, grizzled with black ticking in the southwestern Cape and a lighter whitish grey with greyish ticking in Botswana. **Size** Length 45–60cm; mass 1.5–4.5kg. **Habitat** Distributional ranges overlap, but there are marked differences between the habitat requirements of the two species. The Cape hare prefers dry, open country (notably grassland plains); the scrub hare, scrub or woodland. **Habits** Predominantly nocturnal; hares lie up during the day in grass clumps or under small bushes, which creates depressions or forms with a characteristic shape. They are for the most part solitary. **Food** Leaves, stems and rhizomes of dry and green grass. The Cape hare favours areas with short grass, green grass and fresh green shoots. **Spoor** These animals, which leave a characteristic bounding trail (see illustration below), have a thick mass of hair beneath their feet, so the pad imprints are not well defined. Four claws may show in the spoor of the fore- and hind feet.

Scrub hare

right hind foot

left hind foot

┐0
┘4cm

right forefoot

left forefoot

┐0
┘3.5cm

46

Rock Dassie (Hyrax) *Procavia capensis*

The upperparts of this little animal vary in colour from yellowish buff to reddish or greyish brown; the appearance is generally grizzled. **Size** Length 45–60cm; mass 2.5–4.6kg. **Habitat** The rock dassie occurs only in rocky outcrops. **Habits** Active mainly during the day, lying on rocks in the sun to warm up before starting to feed. They will move 50 or 100m on flat ground to feed. **Food** A browser in some parts of the region, predominantly a grazer in other parts. Usually feeds on the ground, often in bushes. Will also climb trees to feed on leaves, bark and fruits. **Spoor** The dassie has four toes on the front feet and three on the hind. All the toes have nails except the inner one on the hind foot, which has a curved grooming claw that shows in the print. Other signs: Urinates and defecates in latrines.

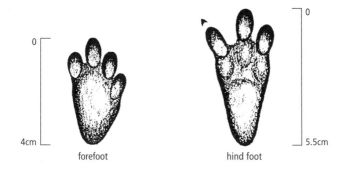

forefoot   hind foot

Temminck's Ground Pangolin *Smutsia (Manis) temminckii*

An unusual animal, armoured with sharp-edged scales.
Size Length 70–100cm; mass 5–15kg. **Habitat** Savanna.
Habits Solitary; predominantly nocturnal. Under severe
stress it curls up into a tight ball. **Food** Ants and termites.
Spoor Five toes on the forefeet, the first with a small nail,
the central three with long, strongly curved claws. Five toes on the hind feet,
each with a short nail-like claw which marks in the spoor. When walking, the
body is balanced on the hind feet, with the forefeet and tail held clear of the
ground. The spoor shows the rounded pads of the hind feet with, usually,
four nails touching the ground, the occasional scrape of the tail and the mark
of the front edges of the long, curved front claws. **Other signs:** Droppings
are usually composed of sand and the remains of ants and termites.

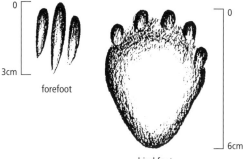

0

3cm

forefoot

0

6cm

hind foot

Southern Lesser Galago (Bushbaby) *Galago moholi*

This little prosimian primate has huge eyes and large, mobile ears. Coloration of the upperparts is light grey or grey-brown; the underparts are somewhat lighter. **Size** Length 30–40cm; mass 120–210g. **Habitat** Savanna woodland, including riverine woodland. **Habits** Nocturnal; rests by day in family groups of two to seven, but usually forages alone by night. May construct a platform-like nest. **Food** Lives on a diet of gum or exuding sap from trees, augmented by insects. **Spoor** Five digits on each foot, with soft, enlarged pads under the tip of each. Apart from the second digit of the hind foot, which has a curved grooming claw, each digit has a small nail. On the ground it moves by hopping on its hind legs, the forelimbs making no contact with the ground.

left hind foot   right hind foot

Vervet Monkey *Chlorocebus pygerythrus*

This little black-faced primate's upperparts are grizzled, the underparts whitish. **Size** Length 95–130cm; mass 3.5–8kg. **Habitat** Mainly savanna woodland. **Habits** Diurnal; active from dawn till mid-morning, when it rests in a sheltered area until early in the afternoon (in hot weather), after which it continues foraging. Spends much of its time in trees searching for wild fruits, but also feeds on the ground. Troops comprise up to 20 members. **Food** Predominantly vegetarian, living on wild fruits, flowers, leaves, seeds and seed pods; also eats insects. **Spoor** Thumb and big toe are fully opposable; each finger and toe has a nail. The feet are larger than the hands.

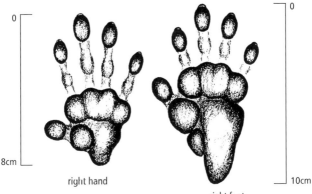

right hand

right foot

Sykes's Monkey *Cercopithecus albogularis*

The Sykes's monkey, also referred to as the Samango monkey, is much darker in colour than the vervet monkey, and has a dark brown (not black) face and long cheek-hairs. **Size** Length 1–1.4m; mass 4–10kg. **Habitat** Forest. **Habits** Diurnal; active from or just before sunrise, but rests during the hottest hours of the day. Troop size varies from four individuals to more than 30. **Food** Mainly fruits, dry and green leaves, flowers, pods and shoots; also eats insects. **Spoor** Identical to that of the vervet monkey, with five fingers on each hand and five toes on each foot.

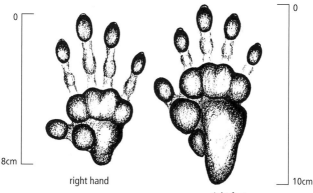

right hand

right foot

Chacma Baboon   *Papio ursinus*

This is the largest of southern Africa's primates (other than humans). Chacma baboons are formidable, especially the males: their canines are longer than those of lion.
Size Length 1–1.6m; mass 25–45kg. **Habitat** Widely distributed; primarily savanna environment but also in mountainous areas and on forest fringes. **Habits** A gregarious species; usually associated with impala herds; troops may number up to 100 individuals. Diurnal; at night they sleep on high krantzes or in trees with thick foliage. **Food** Omnivorous; diet includes grasses, seeds, roots, bulbs, leaves, flowers, wild fruits, pods and shoots. Turns over stones in search of insects, arachnids and slugs. **Spoor** The thumb and big toe are fully opposable; each finger and toe has a nail. The feet are twice as long as the hands. **Other signs:** A very loud bark when alarmed or excited.

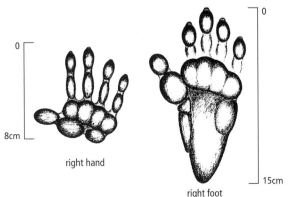

right hand

right foot

Cape Clawless Otter   *Aonyx capensis*

The largest of Africa's otters. The upperparts vary from light to very dark brown, the underparts are lighter in colour. **Size** Length 1.1–1.6m; mass 10–18kg. **Habitat** A predominantly aquatic species. Needs fresh water, even in coastal areas. **Habits** Generally solitary, but also seen in pairs and family parties. Mainly crepuscular. **Food** Mostly crabs, frogs and fish. **Spoor** The otter has five toes on each of the fore- and hind feet. The toes, adapted for feeling and grasping, have no claws on the forefeet and only rudimentary nails on the hind feet. In soft mud, the five toes, the intermediate pads and the proximal pads show clearly in the spoor. Latrines, found near water, are characterized by crabshell remains and fish scales. The droppings can be distinguished from those of the water mongoose (see page 64), whose scats contain rodent fur and other items not normally eaten by otters. Identification is difficult where both species are feeding extensively on crabs alone. The water mongoose, however, invariably leaves the carapace.

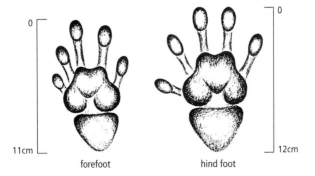

0

0

11cm

12cm

forefoot

hind foot

53

Spotted-necked Otter   *Hydrictis maculicollis*

A much smaller and slimmer animal than the Cape clawless otter (see page 53). Colour varies from chocolate brown to a deep, rich, reddish brown; the throat and upper chest are mottled with white or creamy white. **Size** Length 1m; mass 3–5kg. **Habitat** An aquatic species, closely confined to large rivers, lakes and swamps. **Habits** Usually found solitary or in family parties. Apparently crepuscular. **Food** Mainly fish; also crabs and freshwater molluscs, some birds and some insects. **Spoor** Five toes on the fore- and hind feet; the feet are fully webbed. In soft mud the five toes, the intermediate pads and the proximal pads show clearly in the spoor. The front foot's claws, which are up to 1cm over the curve, are light and very sharp; those on the back feet slightly shorter. You may find it difficult to discern the claw marks in soft mud, and only slight indications of the webs will be apparent, even on close inspection. Nor will the marks be clear on firm substrate. **Other signs:** Defecates and urinates in secluded, sheltered latrines close to the water's edge.

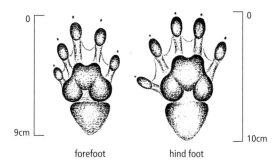

0 · · · 9cm   forefoot

0 · · · 10cm   hind foot

Honey Badger (Ratel) *Mellivora capensis*

A distinctive animal, this stocky, short-legged badger has a broad, light-coloured saddle which runs from above the eyes to the base of the tail, the colour contrasting with the black lower parts of the body. The black bushy tail is often held erect when walking. **Size** Length 90–100cm; mass 8–14kg. **Habitat** Wide tolerance (it is found everywhere except in true desert). **Habits** Predominantly nocturnal; generally solitary, though two or more individuals may hunt together. The animal is normally shy and retiring but it has a well-deserved reputation for ferocity and fearlessness. When under stress it may secrete a strong-smelling fluid. **Food** Omnivorous; diet includes scorpions, spiders, mice, lizards, centipedes, grasshoppers, small birds, snakes, berries, fruits, bee larvae and honey. **Spoor** Five toes on both fore- and hind feet; the claws on the front foot are elongated and powerful; the claws on the hind foot are much shorter. The intermediate pads are fused; a proximal pad on each of the fore- and hind feet is characteristic of the spoor.

0

11cm

0

8cm

forefoot   hind foot

African Striped Weasel   *Poecilogale albunicha*

A slender, sinuous little animal with a bushy tail and four distinctively white, longitudinal stripes on the jet-black fur. **Size** Length 40–50cm; mass 200–350g. **Habitat** A savanna species, largely associated with grassland. **Habits** Striped weasels are mainly nocturnal; generally solitary but also found in pairs and family parties. **Food** Carnivorous; feeds on prey such as mice. **Spoor** Five toes on the fore- and hind feet; the claws on the front foot are strongly curved and longer than those on the hind foot. The proximal pad of the forefoot may sometimes appear in the spoor; the hind-foot spoor will show the outer four toes and claws. The first toe or claw, or both, may also show.

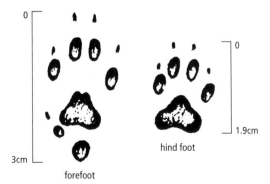

forefoot

hind foot

Striped Polecat *Ictonyx striatus*

A small black animal with distinctive longitudinal white stripes on the sides of its body. The tail is mostly white. **Size** Length 57–67cm, mass 600–1,400g. **Habitat** Wide habitat tolerance. **Habits** Nocturnal, terrestrial and solitary, although also in pairs and groups of females and their young. If cornered, the polecat will turn its hindquarters to the aggressor and eject a pungent secretion from its anal glands. **Food** Mainly insects and mice. **Spoor** Five toes on the fore- and hind feet. The forefoot's claws are strong, curved and long (up to 18mm over the curve); those of the hind feet are much shorter. All five toes and claws on the fore- and hind feet mark in the spoor. The forefoot's proximal pad does not show.

forefoot   hind foot

African Civet   *Civettictis civeta*

The civet has a greyish or whitish shaggy coat with black spots on the body and black stripes on the tail and neck. The lower parts of the legs are black, the tail bushy. **Size** Length 1.2–1.4m; mass 9–15kg. **Habitat** Well-watered savanna and forest. **Habits** Predominantly nocturnal; generally solitary. **Food** Omnivorous; diet includes insects, wild fruits, mice, reptiles, birds, amphibia, myriapods (centipedes and millipedes), arachnids and carrion. **Spoor** Five toes on fore- and hind feet, but only four show in the spoor. The claws make clear marks. The animal deposits its faeces in latrines (or 'civetrenes').

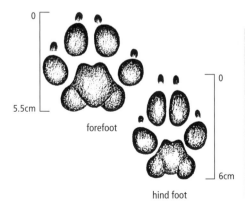

0

5.5cm

forefoot

0

6cm

hind foot

Small-spotted Genet   *Genetta genetta*

Distinguished from the common large-spotted genet (see page 60) by a crest of black hair along the back, a longer and coarser coat, more black on the hind feet, darker body spots and (usually) a white-tipped tail. Its sharp, curved, extendible claws do not show in the spoor. **Size** Length 86–100cm; mass 1.5–2.6kg. **Habitat** The more open areas of savanna woodland, dry grassland and dry vlei areas. **Habits** Nocturnal; mainly solitary, but also found in pairs. **Food** Small rodents, birds, reptiles, insects, spiders and scorpions. **Spoor** Identical to the common large-spotted genet. Five toes on fore- and hind feet; the first is set back and does not show in the footprints; nor do the sharp, curved, extendible claws.

forefoot

hind foot

59

Common Large-spotted Genet   *Genetta maculata*

Similar to the small-spotted genet (see page 59) but lacks the spinal crest and has a black-tipped tail. The spots on the body are generally larger than those of its small-spotted cousin. **Size** Length 85–110cm; mass 1.5–3.2kg. **Habitat** Associated with well-watered country; its presence in arid regions is usually confined to riverine strips. **Habits** Nocturnal; mainly solitary, but also found in pairs. **Food** Rats, mice, insects, ground birds, arachnids, reptiles and wild fruits. **Spoor** Identical to small-spotted genet. Shows four toes in the spoor.

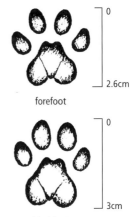

forefoot

0

2.6cm

hind foot

0

3cm

Large Grey Mongoose   *Herpestes ichneumon*

A grey animal covered by coarse fur and a long tail with a distinctive black tip. Lower parts of the legs are black. **Size** Length 1–1.1m; mass 2.5–4kg. **Habitat** Closely associated with water; occurs in riverine forest or bush, or any thick cover near fresh water. **Habits** Mainly diurnal; solitary, but family groups of up to five individuals may also be seen. **Food** Frogs, fish, crabs, mice, birds, reptiles and insects. Also reputed to raid poultry. **Spoor** Five toes on the fore- and hind foot. The first toe of the forefoot is small and located behind the intermediate pad; the forefoot's other four toes have long claws that mark clearly in the spoor. The proximal pad of the forefoot shows in the spoor when the animal is moving slowly but may not do so when it is trotting or running. The first toe of the hind foot does not usually show, but the first claw may mark in the footprint. The other four toes have claws, which are shorter than those of the forefoot and mark clearly in the spoor.

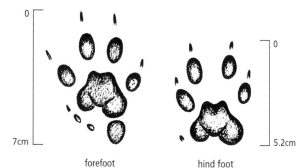

forefoot   hind foot

Slender Mongoose *Galerella sanguinea*

A small, slender animal with a long tail which has a characteristic black tip. Body colour varies, ranging from reddish, yellowish and greyish to a dark brown that looks black in the field. **Size** Length 50–65cm; mass 700–900g. **Habitat** Wide habitat tolerance. **Habits** Terrestrial and solitary; predominantly diurnal. It shelters in disused aardvark holes or holes in termitaria. **Food** Mainly insects; also scorpions, centipedes, lizards, rodents, birds, snakes, frogs and wild fruits. **Spoor** Five toes on the forefoot, the first small and located behind the intermediate pad. Except in soft substrate, the first toe does not (usually) mark in the spoor. The proximal pad of the forefoot, which may show when the animal is moving slowly or in soft substrate, does not show when it is trotting or running. The claws are sharp. The hind foot has five toes, each with a sharp, curved claw; four toes show in the spoor; the fifth does not show but its claw may.

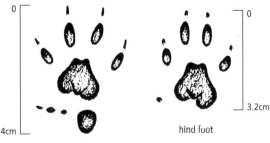

forefoot

hind foot

62

Cape Grey Mongoose   *Galerella pulverulenta*

A small, slim animal, but heavier and more stoutly built than the slender mongoose (see opposite page). Its general colour is speckled grey with the legs darker than the rest of the body. **Size** Length 55–69cm; mass 500g–1kg.
Habitat Wide habitat tolerance. **Habits** Diurnal; normally solitary, occasionally found in pairs and family groups. **Food** Mainly insects, but also wild fruits, carrion, rats, mice, reptiles and ground birds, their eggs and young. **Spoor** Five toes on the forefeet, the first small and located behind the intermediate pad. Except in soft substrate, the first toe does not usually mark in the spoor. The proximal pad of the forefoot, which may show when the animal is moving slowly or in soft substrate, does not mark when it is trotting or running. The hind foot has five toes, but the first toe does not show, although its claw may. The other four toes each have a sharp, curved claw.

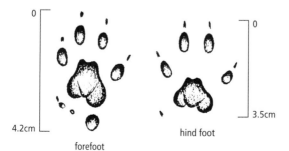

forefoot

hind foot

Water Mongoose   *Atilax paludinosus*

A robust mongoose with a coarse, shaggy coat and tapering tail. Usually dark brown in colour. **Size** Length 80–100cm; mass 2.5–5.5kg. **Habitat** Found near rivers, streams, marshes, swamps, vleis, dams and tidal estuaries. **Habits** Crepuscular. Normally solitary; adult females may be accompanied by juveniles. **Food** Frogs, crabs, rodents, fish, insects, freshwater mussels and vegetable matter. **Spoor** Five toes on the fore- and hind feet, the first small and showing in the spoor behind the intermediate pads. The other four toes are long and finger-like, and tend to splay. Claws on the front feet are stout and curved; those on the back are slightly longer. The proximal pad of the front foot, which may show in the spoor when the animal is moving slowly, may not mark at speed. Dry carapaces of crabs left on river banks are an indication of this mongoose's presence.

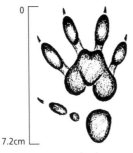

forefoot

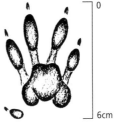

hind foot

Dwarf Mongoose *Helogale parvula*

Africa's smallest mongoose. From a distance the general colour, a uniform speckled brown, appears very dark brown. **Size** Length 35–40cm; mass 220–350g. **Habitat** Favours dry, open woodland or grassland. **Habits** Active only when the sun is well up. Lives in troops of 8–10 individuals; groups take up permanent residence, usually in termite mounds. **Food** Mainly insectivorous; also eats snails, earthworms, reptiles and eggs of ground birds and snakes. **Spoor** Five toes on the forefoot, the first small and located behind the intermediate pad. The forefoot's first toe and proximal pad, which may show when the animal is moving slowly, may not show at speed. The hind foot has five toes but the first toe does not show, although its claw may, positioned well behind the other four toes. The claws of the front feet are long, curved and sharp; those on the hind feet are shorter.

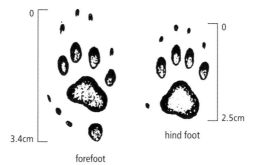

0

0

3.4cm

2.5cm

forefoot

hind foot

65

Banded Mongoose *Mungos mungo*

A small, distinctive mongoose with a coarse, wiry, brownish grey coat. Distinguished by its short, tapering tail and the dozen or so black transverse bands on its back. **Size** Length 50–65cm; mass 1–1.6kg. **Habitat** Wide habitat tolerance.

Habits Diurnal; gregarious; lives in troops that vary in size from a few to more than 30 individuals. **Food** Insects, grubs, myriapods, snails, small reptiles, the eggs and young of ground-nesting birds and wild fruits; also scorpions and spiders. **Spoor** Five toes on the forefoot, the first one small and located behind the intermediate pad. The forefoot's first toe and proximal pad, which may show when the animal is moving slowly, may not do so at speed. Five toes on the hind foot, but the first toe doesn't show, only its claw may, well behind the other four toes. The claws of the front feet are long and sharply curved; those of the back feet are shorter.

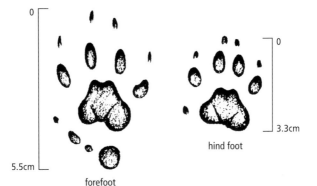

0

5.5cm

forefoot

0

3.3cm

hind foot

White-tailed Mongoose   *Ichneumia albicauda*

A large, shaggy-coated mongoose that is distinguished by its longish legs and a tail that is white for about four-fifths of its length. **Size** Length 90–150cm; mass 3.5–5.2kg. **Habitat** Associated with savanna woodland in well-watered areas. **Habits** Nocturnal; terrestrial (it cannot climb trees). Normally solitary, but also found in pairs and family parties. **Food** Mainly insects; also vegetable matter, millipedes, spiders, scorpions, reptiles, frogs and mice. **Spoor** Five toes on the fore- and hind feet, but the first toes do not show in the spoor. The first claw of the forefoot marks well behind the other four toes; the first claw of the hind foot barely touches the ground. The forefoot's claws are broad, strong and curved; those on the back feet are about the same length but narrower and straighter.

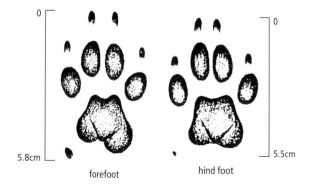

forefoot   hind foot

Yellow Mongoose   *Cynictis penicillata*

A small mongoose with a short, pointed muzzle. Its colour varies from a rich tawny-yellow in the southern parts of the range to grizzled and greyish in the north. The former has a long, white-tipped tail and long-haired coat, the latter a shorter tail without the white tip. **Size** Length 40–60cm; mass 450–900g. **Habitat** Open country. **Habits** Predominantly diurnal; gregarious, living in warrens in colonies of up to 20 or more individuals. **Food** Mainly insectivorous, but also takes mice, small birds, reptiles, scorpions, centipedes, spiders and frogs. **Spoor** Five toes on the forefoot and four on the hind. The forefoot's first toe is set well behind the other four and does not mark in the spoor; nor, usually, does the claw of the first toe. The other four toes have long claws; those on the hind feet are shorter.

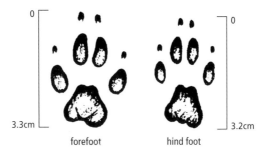

0   0

3.3cm   3.2cm

forefoot   hind foot

Suricate (Meerkat) *Suricata suricatta*

A small, attractive mongoose with conspicuous black rings around the eyes and a slender, tapering, black-tipped tail. Its general colour is a light grizzled fawn with dark brown transverse bands on the back. The animal is commonly known as the meerkat. **Size** Length 45–55cm; mass 620–960g. **Habitat** Occurs throughout the southwestern arid zone. **Habits** Diurnal; gregarious; lives in warrens with several entrances, in colonies of up to 30 individuals. **Food** Mainly insects; also scorpions, spiders millipedes, centipedes and small reptiles. **Spoor** Four toes on the fore- and hind feet. The claws on the front feet are strong and curved; the back ones are much shorter.

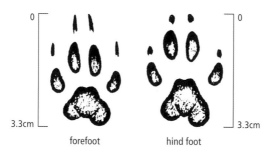

forefoot   hind foot

Bat-eared Fox *Otocyon megalotis*

This attractive animal, which looks rather like a small jackal, has large, black-edged ears, blackish legs and a bushy, black-tipped tail. The overall colour is silvery buffy grey. **Size** Length 75–90cm; mass 3–5kg. **Habitat** Especially associated with open country within the southwest arid and southern savanna zones. **Habits** Both diurnal and nocturnal. **Food** Mainly insects, in particular the harvester termite; also scorpions, murids, mice, reptiles, spiders, millipedes, centipedes and wild fruits. **Spoor** Five toes on the forefoot, the first located far back so that it does not mark in the spoor. The claws on the forefeet are long and slightly curved. Four toes on the hind feet, with short claws. **Other signs:** The holes which it digs when feeding are characteristically narrow and deep.

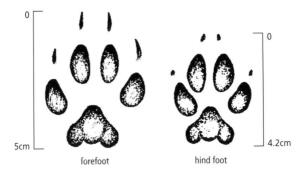

forefoot   hind foot

Cape Fox   *Vulpes chama*

A small fox with large, pointed ears, and a short, pointed muzzle. Its upperparts appear silvery grey, the underparts pale buffy. The bushy tail is pale tawn with a black tip. **Size** Length 86–97cm; mass 2.5–4kg. **Habitat** Found throughout the drier parts of southern Africa. Associated with open grassland and arid scrub; also Cape fynbos. **Habits** Mainly nocturnal; generally solitary or in pairs. **Food** Predominantly mice and insects; also small mammals, scorpions, spiders, centipedes, birds and eggs, reptiles, carrion, wild fruits and green grass; sometimes accused of killing lambs. **Spoor** Five toes on the forefoot; the first toe and claw do not mark in the spoor. Four toes on the hind foot. The claws on both the front and hind feet are thin and sharp.

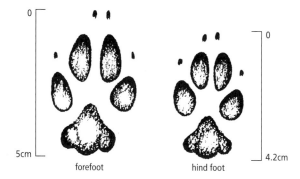

forefoot   hind foot

Black-backed Jackal   *Canis mesomelas*

This animal has a reddish-brown body colour, a black saddle on the back, and a bushy, black-tipped tail. **Size** Length 96–110cm; mass 6–10kg. **Habitat** Wide habitat tolerance. **Habits** Both diurnal and nocturnal; found alone, in pairs and in family parties. **Food** Mainly carrion, but also small mammals such as rats and mice; insects, vegetable matter, birds, reptiles, sun spiders, scorpions, centipedes and green grass. **Spoor** Five toes on the forefoot; the first toe, which carries the dew claw, is set well back and does not mark in the spoor. The hind feet have four toes. The claws are relatively short. Normally moves at a trot, leaving a trail in which both forefoot tracks lie on one side and both hind foot tracks on the other.

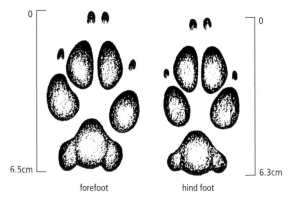

forefoot   hind foot

Side-striped Jackal   *Canis adustus*

A large jackal, overall grey or greyish buff in colour with a white-tipped tail and a faint black-and-white stripe along the side. **Size** Length 96–120cm; mass 7.5–12kg. **Habitat** Avoids open savanna grassland, favouring more thickly wooded country; absent from forest. **Habits** Nocturnal, but sometimes seen early in the morning and in the late afternoon. Found alone, in pairs and in family parties. **Food** Omnivorous; feeds on vegetable matter, wild fruits, small mammals (predominantly rats and mice), insects, carrion, birds and reptiles. **Spoor** Five toes on the front foot; the first toe, which carries the dew claw, is located far back and does not show in the spoor. Four toes on the hind feet.

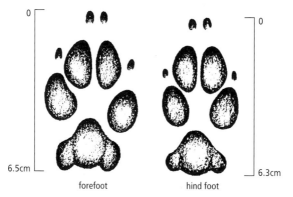

forefoot   hind foot

African Wild Dog *Lycaon pictus*

A dog-like animal in appearance, its body is blotched with black, yellow and white. It has large, rounded ears and a white-tipped bushy tail. **Size** Length 1.05–1.5m; mass 20–30kg. **Habitat** Associated with open plains and open savanna woodland. **Habits** Adapted to living in packs of about 10–15 individuals, though pack size can be up to 50. Hunts by sight, normally in the early morning and late evening. Generally active only during daylight hours. **Food** Mainly smaller to medium-sized antelope; also hares and the young of the larger bovids. **Spoor** Four toes on the fore- and hind feet, each carrying short, powerful claws.

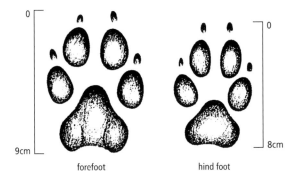

forefoot   hind foot

Aardwolf *Proteles cristatus*

The aardwolf is about the size of a jackal but hyaena-like in shape, with shoulders sloping down to the back legs. It has a thick-haired mane on its back and a bushy, black-tipped tail. It is yellowish brown or buff in colour, with vertical stripes on the body. **Size** Length 84–100cm; mass 6–11kg. **Habitat** Wide tolerance. **Habits** Predominantly nocturnal; normally solitary, but sometimes found in pairs or family parties. **Food** Mainly termites; also other insects, spiders and millipedes. **Spoor** Five toes on the forefoot; the first toe is located high up and does not mark in the spoor. Four toes on the hind feet. The claws are narrow. **Other signs:** The animal defecates within oval-shaped middens; the faeces are covered up by scraping with the front feet.

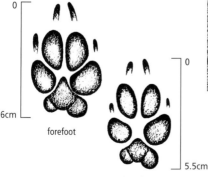

0

6cm

forefoot

0

5.5cm

hind foot

Brown Hyaena   *Hyaena brunnea*

A shy animal, in profile higher at the shoulders than at the rump. Has a long, shaggy brown coat, a lighter-coloured mantle and a long, bushy tail. **Size** Length 1.3–1.6m; mass 42–47kg. **Habitat** Desert, semidesert, open scrub and open woodland savanna. **Habits** Mainly nocturnal; lies in groups but forages alone. **Food** A scavenger, but also hunts small mammals, birds and reptiles. **Spoor** Four toes on the fore- and hind feet, each with a short, heavy claw. Forefoot is much larger than the hind, distinguishing the brown hyaena's spoor from that of its spotted cousin (see opposite page), although the size difference is much less marked in the latter. **Other signs:** Defecates in latrines.

Young animal

0

9.5cm   forefoot

0

7.5cm   hind foot

Old animal

0

10.5cm   forefoot

0

8cm   hind foot

Spotted Hyaena *Crocuta crocuta*

This tough, opportunistic carnivore's shoulders are heavier and stand much higher than its hindquarters; its dull yellowish coat is marked by irregular dark spots. **Size** Length 1.2–1.8m; mass 60–80kg. **Habitat** A savanna species associated with open plains, open woodland and semidesert scrub. **Habits** Social organization is based on a matriarchal system of clans. Predominantly nocturnal, but also active by day. **Food** Mainly large- or medium-sized ungulates, but will hunt or scavenge a wide range of other prey. **Spoor** Four toes on the fore- and hind feet, each with a short, heavy claw. Spoor can be distinguished from that of the brown hyaena (see opposite page) by size difference between fore- and hind feet – a difference more marked in the brown hyaena. **Other signs:** Territorial boundaries are carefully scent-marked with a creamy substance from the anal glands. Defecates in latrines.

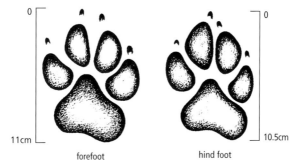

forefoot hind foot

Small Spotted Cat *Felis nigripes*

The smallest of the subregion's cats, generally tawny in colour, marked with large black spots and transverse stripes on the shoulder, with three black bands around the legs. The tail is bushy with a black tip. **Size** Length 50–63cm; mass 1–2kg. **Habitat** Associated especially with open country with some cover. **Habits** Exclusively nocturnal; solitary. **Food** Mainly mice; also spiders, insects, reptiles and birds. **Spoor** Footprints are much smaller than those of any other cats; spoor about the same size as the small-spotted genet's (see page 59), though the shape of the toes and intermediate pads is different.

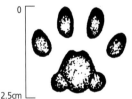

forefoot

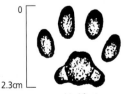

hind foot

Small spotted cat 'scats'

78

African Wild Cat *Felis silvestris cafra*

Looks very much like the domestic cat, but is slightly larger. The general colour ranges from greyish through buffish to ochre-like, with dark spots and stripes. **Size** Length 05–100cm; mass 2.5–6kg. **Habitat** Wide tolerance. **Habits** Nocturnal; solitary. **Food** Mainly rats and mice; also birds, reptiles, insects, spiders and small mammals such as hares, springhares and the young of small antelope. **Spoor** Footprints are similar in shape and size to those of the domestic cat. **Other signs:** Like the domestic cat, it excavates a depression to defecate, and carefully covers the scats by scraping with the front feet.

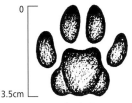

forefoot

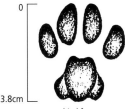

hind foot

79

Serval   *Leptailurus serval*

A slender cat with long legs, small head, large ears and spotted and barred coat. The general colour is yellow with black spots. **Size** Length 96–120cm; mass 8–13kg. **Habitat** Confined to areas where there is permanent water; found in the higher rainfall areas. **Habits** Predominantly nocturnal; normally solitary, but also sometimes seen in pairs and family groups (females with young). **Food** Preys mainly on rats and mice; also other small mammals, birds, frogs, small reptiles, insects and sun spiders. **Spoor** Footprints similar to those of the caracal (see opposite page), but narrower, the indentation at the front of the intermediate pad not as prominent. **Other signs:** Drops scats randomly along paths, usually choosing a patch of short grass or a depression. It takes little or no trouble to cover the scats, making no more than a few quick scratches with the hind feet.

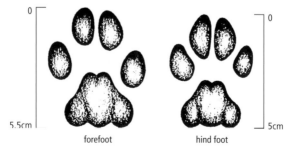

0 — 5.5cm

forefoot

0 — 5cm

hind foot

Caracal   *Caracal caracal*

A stockier cat than the serval (see opposite page) with shorter limbs, a short bushy tail and characteristic tufts on the ears. The overall colour is a reddish tan. **Size** Length 70–110cm; mass 7–19kg. **Habitat** Associated with open savanna woodland, open grassland and vleis. **Habits** Mostly nocturnal; solitary. **Food** Mainly small and medium-sized prey, which includes monkeys, the young of the larger antelopes, dassies, birds and reptiles. **Spoor** Footprints are broader than those of the serval, and the indentation at the front of the intermediate pads is more prominent.

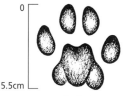

0

5.5cm

forefoot

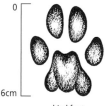

0

6cm

hind foot

Note the heavy indentation at the front of the intermediate pads.

81

Cheetah *Acinonyx jubatus*

A more slender animal than the leopard (see page 84), with longer legs, a much smaller head, and characteristic black 'tear marks' from the eye to the mouth. Its spots are also much smaller and more rounded than the leopard's rosettes. **Size** Length 1.8–2.2m; mass 40–60kg. **Habitat** Open plains, the more open areas within savanna woodland, and the fringes of deserts. **Habits** Predominantly diurnal; at its most active around sunrise and sunset;

Adult cheetah footprint: note the extended claws.

relies on speed to catch prey. Occurs in pairs or family parties of three or four, and to a lesser extent solitary males. **Food** Mainly medium-sized or small bovids or the young of larger bovids; also terrestrial birds and small mammals such as hares and porcupines. **Spoor** Unlike those of other cats, the cheetah's claws do not retract into sheaths but remain extended at all times. Longitudinal ridges beneath these high-speed predator's intermediate pads act like tyre-treads to prevent skidding.

forefoot   hind foot

Leopard   *Panthera pardus*

A more solid-bodied animal than the cheetah (see page 82), with shorter, stockier legs, and a larger head. Coloration is golden yellow, with distinct black, light-centred rosettes. **Size** Length 1.6–2.1m; mass 20–90kg. **Habitat** Wide tolerance. **Habits** Solitary, except during the mating season or when female is accompanied by young. Mainly nocturnal, with some diurnal activity in undisturbed areas. **Food** Catholic diet includes small to medium-sized ungulates; on occasion larger mammals such as kudu and hartebeest. Also eats dassies, rats, mice, hares, birds, snakes, lizards, insects, scorpions, some of the smaller carnivores and occasionally baboons. Will also scavenge. **Spoor** Male's footprints are larger and proportionately broader than those of the female. Female's toes are more slender. The leopard extends its claws only

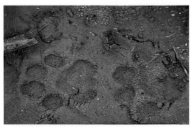

when alarmed or charging. **Other signs:** Both males and females scent-mark by spraying urine. Leaves marks on trees where it has climbed or sharpened its claws. Traces of blood on the tree and animal remains indicate a carcass has been dragged up into the branches.

The leopard's droppings: old (left) and new (right)

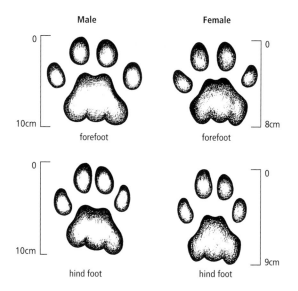

Lion   *Panthera leo*

Largest of Africa's carnivores, sandy or tawny in colour; the males carry a mane of thick hair around the neck. **Size** Length 2.5–3.3m; mass 110–225kg. **Habitat** Wide tolerance. **Habits** Mainly nocturnal; also active around sunrise and towards sunset and sometimes during daylight hours. The animal lives and hunts in prides which may number from a few individuals to 30 or more. Solitary males ousted from prides; solitary subadult males and females may also occur and tend to be nomadic. **Food** Mainly medium-sized to large ungulates, but will kill a wide variety of mammals, from buffalo down to mice; also birds, reptiles and even insects. **Spoor** The male's footprints are larger and proportionately broader than those of the female; the female's toes are more slender than those of the male (a young male's footprints may be the same size as a female's but can be distinguished by the shape). The claws are extended when charging, and show in the spoor. **Other signs:** The lion scent-marks by spraying urine against shrubs, and at the same time makes scrape marks on the ground. It also sharpens its claws, and leaves claw marks, on the bark of trees.

Lion droppings

Spoor of an adult male lion

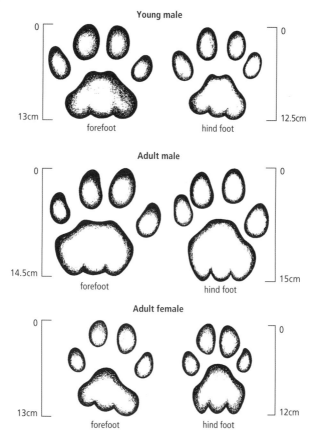

Young male

0

13cm

forefoot

0

12.5cm

hind foot

Adult male

0

14.5cm

forefoot

0

15cm

hind foot

Adult female

0

13cm

forefoot

0

12cm

hind foot

African (Bush) Elephant   *Loxodonta africana*

The world's largest living land mammal, boasting a flexible and multipurpose trunk used for gathering its food, sucking up water, greeting other elephants, chastening youngsters, smelling, trumpeting, breathing, and also as a weapon.

Size Shoulder height 2.5–4m; mass 2.8–6.3 tons. **Habitat** Wide tolerance. **Habits** Gregarious; family groups comprise an adult female with her offspring or a number of closely related females with their offspring. Groups may come together to form herds. Bulls join the family herds only when a female is in oestrus. **Food** Browses and grazes a wide variety of plants. **Spoor** Five hoofed toes on the front feet and four on the hind. The feet have a thick layer of cartilage, which acts as a shock absorber – and enables the elephant to move with minimal sound. The horny soles of the feet are cracked on the surface, the mosaic of cracks marking in the spoor. The random pattern of the cracks makes it possible for a trained tracker to identify individual elephants. The front feet are round and larger than the hind. Some trackers maintain that the hind feet of females, which are oval, are larger than those of males, but this needs to be confirmed. **Other signs:** Elephants can be very destructive in their feeding habits, pushing over trees, pulling them up by the roots, or breaking off branches to get at young, fresh foliage. They also dig holes in sand, on river banks, to drink the clean, filtered water seeping through.

Hind footprint

Elephants dig holes for water.

Droppings

Male

0

50cm

forefoot

0

50cm

hind foot

Female

0

50cm

forefoot

0

58cm

hind foot

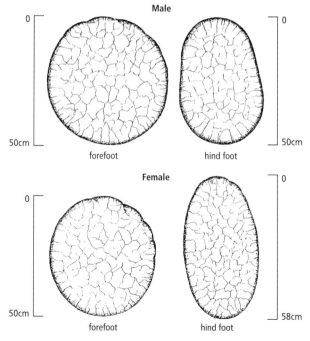

Square-lipped (White) Rhinoceros   *Ceratotherium simum*

Characteristic features of this massive herbivore include the square upper lip and a prominent hump above the shoulders. It is larger in size, and has a longer head, than its cousin the hook-lipped (black) rhinoceros (see page 92). **Size** Shoulder height 1.8m; mass 1.4–2.3 tons. **Habitat** Areas of short grass, with adequately thick bush cover and fairly flat terrain. This rhino is endangered; confined to reserves and other protected areas. **Habits** The animal grazes at night, during the morning and in the late afternoon and evening, resting at intervals of a few hours. During the heat of the day it rests in shade. Occurs in small groups. **Food** Grass. **Spoor** Three toes, each with a broad, stout nail, on the fore- and hind feet. The nails are proportionately bigger, and gaps between them smaller than those of the hook-lipped rhino. The spoor of an adult square-lipped rhino is bigger than that of a hook-lipped rhino. Cushioned pads on the soles of the feet have a hard surface showing an intricate mosaic of irregular cracks – a random pattern from which one can identify individuals. **Other signs:** The species has a preference for short grass, which it crops to within a centimetre of the ground.

The bite width of an adult is about 20cm. Dominant bulls habitually demarcate their territories with latrines and by spray-urinating along the boundaries. The dung of the white rhino contains grass.

Droppings of a square-lipped rhino

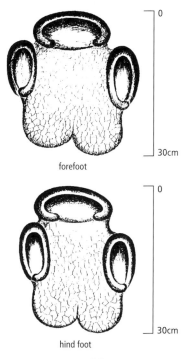

forefoot

hind foot

Hook-lipped (Black) Rhinoceros   *Diceros bicornis*

Distinguished from the square-lipped (white) rhinoceros (see page 90) by its smaller size, pointed upper lip and smaller head. **Size** Shoulder height 1.6m; mass 800–1,100kg. **Habitat** Needs an adequate supply of scrub and young trees on which to browse; also well-developed woodland or thickets where it can shelter during the heat of the day. The hook-lipped rhino is highly endangered; confined to reserves and other protected areas. **Habits** Solitary, or female with calf. Active during the early morning and late afternoon. **Food** Mainly browses, but small quantities of grass are taken during the wet season. **Spoor** Three toes, each with a broad, stout nail, on the fore- and hind feet. The

nails are proportionately smaller than those of square-lipped rhino, the gaps between them bigger. The animal's spoor is also smaller than that of an adult square-lipped rhinoceros. Cushioned pads on the soles of the feet have a hard surface with a mosaic of irregular cracks, creating a random pattern in the spoor from which one can identify individual animals. **Other signs:** A hook-lipped rhino deposits dung in latrines, but will also defecate randomly anywhere in its home range. It also sprays urine, kicks its dung about and spreads it around with its horn, all of which are signposts to its presence in an area. The dung contains twigs and the remains of leaves.

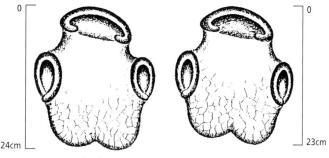

0   0

24cm   23cm

          forefoot   hind foot

Plains Zebra   *Equus quagga*

This common relative of the horse can be distinguished from the two mountain zebras, *Equus zebra* (see opposite page), by the yellowish or greyish shadow stripes between the black on the hindquarters, and also by the absence of a 'gridiron' pattern on top of the rump. **Size** Shoulder height 1.3m; mass 290–340kg. **Habitat** A savanna species, favouring areas of open woodland, open scrub and grassland. **Habits** Generally active throughout the day. Gregarious; lives in small family groups. **Food** Predominantly a grazer, but will sometimes browse and feed on herbs. **Spoor** Hoofprints are a similar shape to, but much smaller than, those of adult horses; larger than those of domestic donkeys. **Other signs:** Droppings have a regular kidney shape.

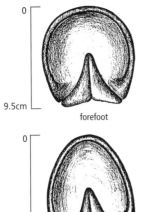

0

9.5cm

forefoot

0

10cm

hind foot

Zebra droppings

Mountain Zebra *Equus zebra*

The two mountain zebras, which are very similar to each other, differ from plains zebra in their smaller body size, black body stripes, which do not continue on to the white underparts, and lack of shadow stripes between the body stripes. The black markings on the rump form a characteristic 'gridiron' pattern. **Size** Shoulder height 1.3m; mass 250–260kg. **Habitat** Historically, the Cape mountain zebra (subspecies *zebra*) occurred throughout the mountainous areas of the Cape (now seen in reserves such as the Mountain Zebra National Park), while Hartmann's mountain zebra (subspecies *hartmannae*) has been restricted to mountainous areas and flats in Namibia. **Habits** Mainly diurnal; gregarious. **Food** Predominantly a grazer, but will also browse. **Spoor** The hoofprints of adult mountain zebra are smaller than those of adult plains zebra. The hoofprints of the two subspecies of mountain zebra are identical but, as their distribution does not overlap, cannot be confused.

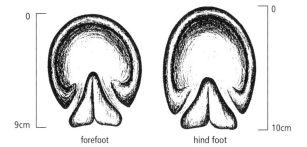

Cape mountain zebra

forefoot   hind foot

Hippopotamus   *Hippopotamus amphibius*

This huge animal is especially adapted for its aquatic life: eyes, nose and ears all protrude from the water when the rest of the animal is submerged. **Size** Shoulder height 1.5m; mass 1–2 tons. **Habitat** Needs open water in which it can totally submerge. **Habits** A nocturnal feeder; rests by day partially submerged. Gregarious; occurs in herds (or schools), usually of between 10 and 15 individuals. **Food** Grass. **Spoor** Has four toes, each with heavy broad nails, on the fore- and hind feet. Hippos tend to use established routes on dry land, the ground eventually being worn deeply into narrow paths. These are grooved on either side by the feet, leaving a narrow raised central ridge of loose soil. **Other signs:** Territories are marked by piles of faeces, which the hippo scatters over a bush or stone by flicking its tail from side to side.

forefoot

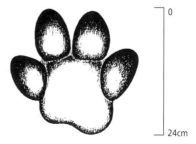

hind foot

Giraffe   *Giraffa camelopardalis*

There are several varieties of this, the world's tallest animal, in Africa, each with a distinctive reticulate (net-like) pattern. The head has horny projections which the male uses, when fighting, to strike at the legs and neck of its opponent.

On these occasions the two combatants stand side on and swing their long necks in wide arcs. The long, rough tongue enables the giraffe to grasp foliage and to strip the leaves of acacias; the copious, viscous saliva it produces helps it to swallow the thorns. The animal can gallop at up to 60km/h but usually defends itself by kicking. **Size** Shoulder height 3.9–5.2m; mass 970–1,400kg. **Habitat** Associated with a wide variety of dry savanna

ranging from scrub to woodland; often seen in company with zebra and wildebeest, who benefit from the giraffe's height and ability to survey the horizon. **Habits** Predominantly diurnal. Gregarious, a loose herd structure comprises females and young, bachelor or mixed groups. Bulls are for the most part solitary. **Food** Browser; favours acacia leaves and flowers. **Spoor** Footprints are much larger and longer than those of any other of the cloven-hoofed animals. **Other signs:** Droppings have one pointed end and an indentation at the blunt end, and are usually scattered by the height from which they fall. Saliva in the upper parts of trees may indicate the animal's very recent presence.

Droppings are usually scattered.

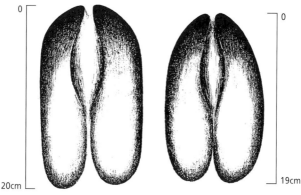

forefoot

hind foot

Common Warthog   *Phacochoerus aethiopicus*

An unmistakable pig-like animal with characteristic tusks, and wart-like protuberances on the face. Skin colour, often determined by the colour of the mud in which it wallows, is generally grey. **Size** Shoulder height 70cm; mass 60–105kg. **Habitat** Grassland, floodplains, vleis and other open areas, including open woodland. **Habits** Diurnal; groups, called sounders, consist of an adult male, adult female and her offspring. Maternity and bachelor groups, and solitary individuals, are also found. **Food** Generally vegetarian. **Spoor** The hooves are narrower than those of bushpigs (see opposite page); the dew claws usually mark clearly in the spoor. **Other signs:** Defecates randomly, and is prone to rubbing itself against any convenient object. Often wallows in mud.

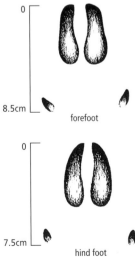

0

8.5cm

forefoot

0

7.5cm

hind foot

Warthog droppings

Bushpig *Potamochoerus larvatus*

The overall colour varies, but it is commonly reddish brown, with a dorsal crest of long, white hair. **Size** Shoulder height 55–88cm; mass 60–115kg. **Habitat** Forest, reed beds, riverine woodland and dense bush. **Habits** Predominantly nocturnal, with some daytime activity. Gregarious; they move in groups of six to eight. **Food** Omnivorous. **Spoor** Hooves are broader than those of warthogs (see opposite page), and the dew claws usually mark clearly in the spoor. Consistently uses the same routes to feeding areas, thereby forming narrow, clearly marked paths. **Other signs:** Practises tree-marking by tusking; defecates in latrines.

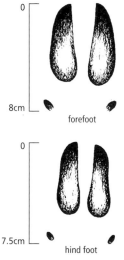

0

8cm

forefoot

0

7.5cm

hind foot

Aardvark   *Orycteropus afer*

This unusual mammal has a humped back, long pig-like snout, long donkey-like ears and a thick, tapering tail. **Size** Length 1.4–1.8m; mass 40– 70kg. **Habitat** Wide tolerance. **Habits** It is almost exclusively nocturnal; generally solitary, although pairs (at mating time) and females with young are seen. **Food** Mainly termites in summer, ants in winter. **Spoor** Four toes on the forefeet, five on the hind. The toes are armed with stout, broad claws. The front footprints show three toes and their claws: the first toe is absent, and only the tip of the fifth claw marks in the spoor. The hind footprint shows the three middle toes and claws, and only the tips of the first and fifth claws mark in the spoor. The hind footprints usually lie close behind or slightly overlie the front ones. **Other signs:** Apart from small exploratory scratchings, the aardvark makes three types of excavations: shallow diggings to gain access to food; shallow, temporary refuges that may run several metres underground; and a much more permanent structure used as a shelter in which the young are born. These shelters often have an extensive burrow system with several entrances. Unoccupied burrows provide shelter and safe refuge for a wide variety of mammals, birds, reptiles and insects. The aardvark buries its faeces and does not use latrines; the droppings are ovoid and consist mainly of sand and other indigestible matter.

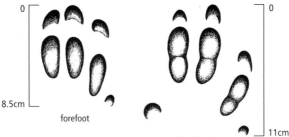

forefoot

hind foot

Blue Duiker *Philantomba monticola*

Southern Africa's smallest antelope, distinguished by its large eyes and slim legs. Colour of the upperparts varies: it can be a dark smokey brown with a dark bluish sheen, rusty brown, or dark brown. Both sexes carry tiny horns. **Size** Shoulder height 35cm; mass 4kg. **Habitat** Confined to forests, thickets and dense coastal bush. **Habits** Usually solitary; active in the early morning and after sunset. **Food** Browses freshly fallen forest-floor leaves. **Spoor** Creates well-marked paths on its routes between its resting, feeding and drinking places.

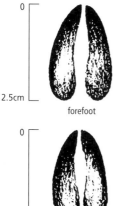

0

2.5cm

forefoot

0

2.3cm

hind foot

Natal Red Duiker *Cephalophus natalensis*

This attractive little antelope has chestnut red or orange-red upperparts. Both sexes carry the short, straight horns. **Size** Shoulder height 43cm; mass 10–16kg. **Habitat** Associated with forest and dense thicket near water. **Habits** Solitary, or female with offspring. Mainly active at night. **Food** A browser of leaves, shoots, fruits and berries. **Spoor/Signs** Uses communal dung heaps.

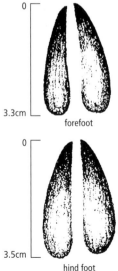

0

3.3cm

forefoot

0

3.5cm

hind foot

Common Duiker *Sylvicapra grimmia*

This smallish antelope, whose colour varies from a grizzled grey to a yellowish fawn, has a characteristic black band running from nose to forehead. Only the males carry horns, which are short and straight. **Size** Shoulder height 50cm; mass 18–21kg. **Habitat** Needs bush for shelter, shade and food. Wide tolerance; has a preference for savanna woodland. **Habits** Solitary; found in pairs when females are in oestrus; also female with single young. Mainly active in the early morning, and late afternoon – extending well into the night. **Food** Almost exclusively a browser. **Spoor/Signs** Uses secretions from its facial glands to mark its territory. Droppings are round and pellet-like.

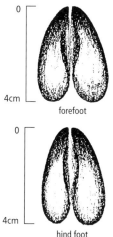

forefoot

hind foot

Pellet-like droppings

Suni *Neotragus moschatus*

The suni's upperparts are rufous-brown with a slightly speckled appearance, and the underparts are white. Only the males carry horns. **Size** Shoulder height 35cm; mass 5kg. **Habitat** Dry woodland, with thicket and underbrush.

Habits Usually solitary, but may be found in pairs or in family groups. Mainly active in the early morning and late afternoon. **Food** A browser. **Spoor/Signs** Uses communal latrines. It also demarcates its territory with secretions from facial glands.

forefoot   hind foot

Damara Dik-dik   *Madoqua damarensis*

The upperparts of this attractive little animal are yellowish grey; only the males carry the small, straight horns. The nose is elongated, mobile and proboscis-like. **Size** Shoulder height 38cm; mass 5kg. **Habitat** Dense woodland and thicket on stony or hard clay ground. **Habits** Single, in pairs or in family groups. Active at sunrise, in the late afternoon and at dusk, with some activity after dark. **Food** Predominantly a browser. **Spoor/Signs** Uses communal dung heaps; a male will paw the old dung into a heap with the forefeet, urinate on it and may paw again before defecating. Afterwards it wipes its preorbital glands on the nearest grass stems or scrubs.

forefoot   hind foot

Sharpe's Grysbok *Raphicerus sharpei*

The body is a rich reddish brown, sprinkled with white hairs. Only the males carry the short horns. **Size** Shoulder height 50cm; mass 7.5kg. **Habitat** Areas of low-growing scrub and grass of medium height. **Habits** Usually single, in pairs, or female with single offspring. Mainly nocturnal but also active in the early morning and late afternoon. **Food** Predominantly a browser. **Spoor/ Signs** Often returns to the same place to deposit droppings, which form heaps.

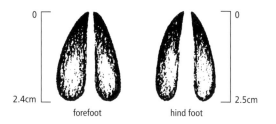

forefoot   hind foot

Cape (Southern) Grysbok   *Raphicerus melanotis*

The grysbok's upperparts are rufous-brown and flecked with white hairs, giving it a grizzled appearance. Only the males have horns. **Size** Shoulder height 54cm; mass 10kg. **Habitat** Thick scrub bush. **Habits** Nocturnal; they are mainly solitary; pairs or females with young are found during the mating period. **Food** Predominantly a grazer. **Spoor/Signs** The grysbok deposits its droppings in dung heaps.

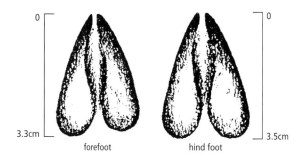

0	0
3.3cm	3.5cm
forefoot	hind foot

Steenbok   *Raphicerus campestris*

The upperparts of the steenbok are reddish brown, the underparts white. Ears very large; only the males carry horns. **Size** Shoulder height 50cm; mass 11kg. **Habitat** Associated with open grassland with some cover; also found in open woodland. **Habits** Solitary, except when the male is attending a female in oestrus, or a female is still with her young. Mainly diurnal; active in the early morning and late evening. **Food** Both a browser and grazer. **Spoor/ Signs** Latrines tend to be near the perimeter of its territory. When defecating or urinating it will clear a spot with the front hooves, defecate or urinate, and then cover up the faeces by scraping soil over them with its front feet.

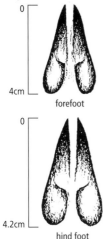

forefoot

hind foot

Steenbok droppings

Oribi *Ourebia ourebi*

The colour of the oribi's upperparts is yellowish rufous; the underparts white. The tail is black and bushy on the upper surface. The neck is longer and thinner than that of the steenbok (see opposite page). Only the males have horns. **Size** Shoulder height 60cm; mass 14kg. **Habitat** Prefers open country, such as open grassland or floodplains. **Habits** Found solitary, in pairs, or in parties comprising male and either one or two females with their offspring. **Food** Predominantly a grazer, but will also browse. **Spoor/Signs** Uses communal dung heaps. Marks grass stems with preorbital glands, leaving a small amount of black secretion.

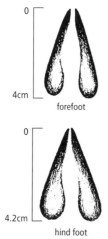

0

4cm

forefoot

0

4.2cm

hind foot

Oribi droppings

Klipspringer   *Oreotragus oreotragus*

The colour of this agile antelope varies from speckled, yellowish brown to greyish brown; the coat has a coarse texture that blends in with the rocks among which it lives. Only the males carry horns. **Size** Shoulder height 60cm; mass 10–13kg. **Habitat** Restricted to a rocky habitat.

Habits Found singly, in pairs, or in small family groups. Browses or grazes on the flatter ground surrounding its habitat, but if disturbed will run for rocky shelter. Active in the early morning and late afternoon. **Food** Predominantly a browser. **Spoor** Walks on the tips of its hooves, which have long, narrow soles and blunt, rounded tips. The rounded hooves are an adaptation to the rocky terrain it inhabits. **Other signs:** Scent-marks by smearing a black, tarry secretion from its preorbital glands onto twigs. Scatters dung heaps throughout its territory; tends to defecate on or near the territorial border.

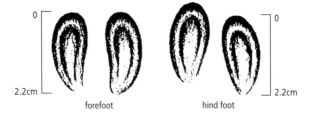

forefoot   hind foot

Springbok *Antidorcas marsupialis*

This medium-sized antelope's back is a bright cinnamon-brown with a broad, dark reddish-brown horizontal band separating the upperparts from the white underparts. Both sexes carry horns. The common name is derived from the way the animal springs or bounds with its back arched to expose a white ridge of hair, a display known as 'pronking' and said to advertise its fitness to other springbok and to predators. **Size** Shoulder height 75cm; mass 37–41kg. **Habitat** Associated with arid regions and open grassland. **Habits** Gregarious. Active in the early morning and late afternoon; some activity after dark. **Food** Both a browser and grazer. **Spoor/Signs** Marks its territory with conspicuous latrines.

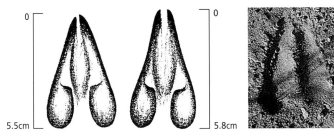

forefoot   hind foot

Impala   *Aepyceros melampus*

The upperparts of this graceful, medium-sized antelope are a rich reddish brown, the flanks reddish pale fawn, the underparts white. Only the males carry horns. Hind legs have black glands just above the hoof, called metatarsals, which are diagnostic. **Size** Shoulder height 90cm; mass 40–50kg. **Habitat** Associated with woodland. **Habits** Gregarious. **Food** Both a browser and grazer. **Spoor/Signs** The male creates dung heaps during the rut (mating season), which are scattered within the territory. At other times both sexes urinate and defecate at random.

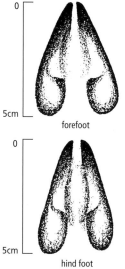

0

5cm

forefoot

0

5cm

hind foot

Grey Rhebok   *Pelea capreolus*

The grey rhebok has a long, slender neck and long, narrow pointed ears. The upperparts of its body and flanks are greyish brown, the underparts white; the hair is short, thick and woolly. Only the males of the species carry horns.
Size Shoulder height 75cm; mass 20kg. **Habitat** Associated with rocky hills, rocky mountain slopes and mountain plateaux with good grass cover. **Habits** Solitary males, and family parties numbering up to 12 individuals can be seen. Active throughout the day. **Food** Grass. **Spoor** Similar to that of mountain reedbuck (see page 116) but slightly narrower and sharper.

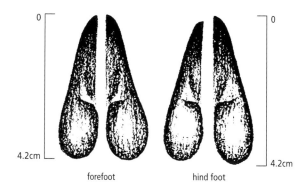

forefoot   hind foot

Mountain Reedbuck   *Redunca fulvorufula*

The upperparts of this medium-sized antelope are greyish and the underparts white. The neck is reddish. The coat is soft and woolly and the tail bushy. The characteristic gland located just below the ears appears as a black patch. Only the males carry the short, heavily ridged, forward-pointing horns. **Size** Shoulder height 72cm; mass 30kg. **Habitat** Dry, grass-covered, stony slopes of hills and mountains where there is cover in the way of bushes or scattered trees. **Habits** Usually occurs in small groups of three to six, but also in herds of up to 30. The animal is at its most active in the early mornings, late afternoons and at night. **Food** Almost exclusively a grazer. **Spoor** Similar to that of the grey rhebok (see page 115) but slightly broader.

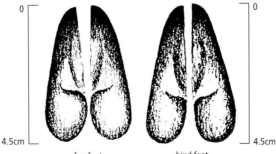

forefoot   hind foot

Common (Southern) Reedbuck   *Redunca arundinum*

The reedbuck's overall body colour varies from brown to grey or buffy grey, yellow or buffy yellow or greyish brown. The back is usually slightly darker; the underparts are white. Only the males carry horns. **Size** Shoulder height 80–95cm; mass 50–70kg. **Habitat** Essential habitat requirements include cover, in the form of tall grass or reedbeds, and a good water supply; usually found in vleis with a wet drainage area or grassland adjacent to streams, rivers or other areas of permanent water. **Habits** Lives in pairs or family parties. **Food** Almost exclusively a grazer. **Spoor/Signs** Tends to use fixed trails leading to water. Before lying down, it will trample the ground, breaking down the grass to form a bed.

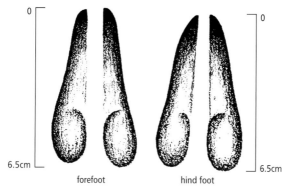

0				0
6.5cm				6.5cm

forefoot   hind foot

Red Lechwe *Kobus leche*

The upperparts of this antelope's body and flanks are reddish yellow, the underparts white, the lower legs black. Only the males carry horns. **Size** Shoulder height 1m; mass 100kg. **Habitat** A water-loving species found in the shallow inundations of floodplains fringing swamps and rivers; and in high-standing beds of papyrus, reeds and semi-aquatic grasses on the fringes of dry land. **Habits** Gregarious; found in small herds of 15–20 individuals. Active before sunrise and in the early morning, and again in the late afternoon and, for a time, after sunset. **Food** Almost exclusively a grazer. **Spoor** The hooves of the lechwe are distinctly elongated, although not so much as those of the sitatunga (see page 121). They splay sideways on soft ground, which helps the animal to negotiate muddy terrain.

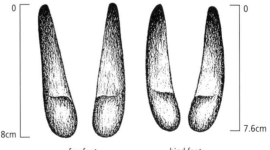

forefoot   hind foot

Puku *Kobus vardonii*

Sometimes confused with the impala (see page 114), but the puku's horns do not spiral. The upperparts of the body are golden yellow, the underparts lighter. Restricted to a narrow stretch in the Caprivi region of Namibia; found nowhere else in southern Africa. Only the males carry horns. **Size** Shoulder height 80cm; mass 62–74kg. **Habitat** Associated with grassy areas in the immediate vicinity of water. **Habits** Gregarious; crepuscular. **Food** Predominantly a grazer. **Spoor** Elongated hoofs, adapted for soft, muddy ground.

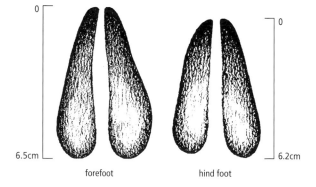

0

6.5cm

forefoot

0

6.2cm

hind foot

Waterbuck   *Kobus ellipsiprymnus*

The colour of this large antelope's upperparts is variable: it may be a dark brownish grey or greyish brown, grizzled with white and grey hairs. A characteristic white ring encircles the rump. Only the males carry horns. **Size** Shoulder height 1.3m; mass 250–270kg. **Habitat** Associated with water. **Habits** Gregarious; active during all but the hottest hours of the day. **Food** Predominantly a grazer, but also browses. **Spoor** Roughly triangular-shaped hoofprints, which are quite characteristic.

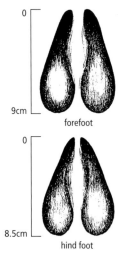

0

9cm

forefoot

0

8.5cm

hind foot

Sitatunga   *Tragelaphus spekii*

Adult males are dark drab brown (females similar, or redder). The hair is long, coarse and shaggy. Only males carry horns. **Size** Shoulder height 90cm; mass 115kg. **Habitat** Usually found in dense papyrus and reedbeds in swamp areas, in water up to a metre deep; sometimes feeds in woodland fringes. **Habits** Semi-aquatic; active most of the day, except during the hottest hours. Occurs in small herds of up to about six individuals. An excellent swimmer. **Food** Aquatic grasses, plants growing in the shallower water, and the freshly sprouting tips of reeds. **Spoor** The adult male sitatunga's elongated, widely splayed hooves may reach a length of up to 18cm on the forefeet and up to 16cm on the hind (the measurements given below are those actually recorded by the author). **Other signs:** Uses established paths when moving from swamp to woodland.

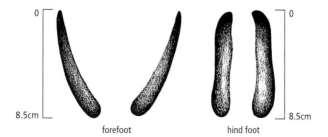

0   0

8.5cm   8.5cm

forefoot   hind foot

Bushbuck   *Tragelaphus sylvaticus*

Individual bushbuck vary widely in size over their range. Their general colour also varies, from chestnut to dark brown. All the animals, however, have a conspicuous white collar, with white spots on the cheeks and flanks. The flanks and hindquarters sometimes show stripes. Only the males carry horns. **Size** Average shoulder height 80cm; mass 45kg. **Habitat** Closely associated with riverine or other types of underbrush close to permanent water. **Habits** Generally solitary; also occurs in small groups of two or three. Active at night, in early morning and late evening. **Food** Mainly a browser, but also grazes. **Spoor** Heart-shaped hoof, similar to that of common duiker (see page 105) but larger.

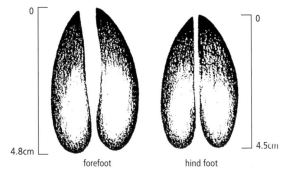

0   0

4.8cm   4.5cm

forefoot   hind foot

Greater Kudu *Tragelaphus strepsiceros*

A large fawn-grey antelope with 6–10 vertical white stripes on the sides. Usually only the males carry horns, which are long and deeply spiralled. **Size** Shoulder height 140–155cm; mass 180–250kg. **Habitat** Savanna woodland. **Habits** Gregarious; occurs in small herds, usually up to four or so individuals. Adult males may be solitary. Most active in the early morning and late afternoon. **Food** A browser. **Spoor** The male's forefoot is proportionally broader than that of the female.

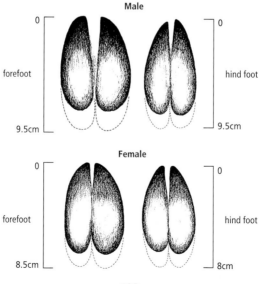

Nyala   *Tragelaphus angasii*

A largish antelope, the sexes markedly different in appearance. The male has a shaggy, greyish coat with a white crest on the back and long hair on the neck, belly and rump, and 9–14 vertical white stripes down its sides. The female also carries the stripes but is much smaller, yellowish brown to chestnut in colour, and lacks the shaggy hair. Only the males carry horns. **Size** Shoulder height 1.15m; mass 62–108kg. **Habitat** Prefers thicket in dry savanna woodland, riverine woodland with thicket, and dry forest. **Habits** Gregarious; occurs in groups of usually two or three individuals, but herds can number up to 30. Solitary males are also common. Both diurnal and nocturnal. **Food** Predominantly a browser. **Spoor** The forefoot of the male is larger and proportionately broader than that of the female.

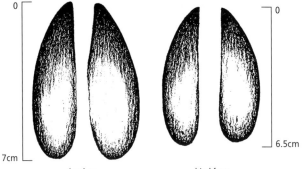

forefoot   hind foot

Common Eland *Taurotragus (Tragelaphus) oryx*

The largest of Africa's antelopes, light rufous-fawn in colour, with narrow white stripes down the flanks. Both sexes carry horns, the male's are much heavier than the female's. **Size** Shoulder height 1.7m; mass 450–700kg. **Habitat** Wide tolerance. **Habits** Occurs in small herds, but occasionally in huge aggregations of more than 1 000. Active in mornings and afternoons. **Food** Mainly a browser, but grazes fresh, sprouting grass after fire. **Spoor** The hind foot is more elongated than that of the buffalo (see page 126) and of domestic cattle.

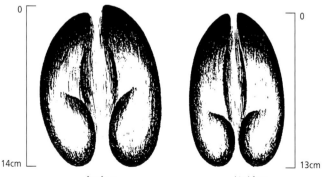

forefoot   hind foot

African Savanna Buffalo   *Syncerus caffer*

A massive animal, ox-like in general appearance. Old males are black; females show a tinge of reddish brown. The curved horns are huge in old adult males; those of the females are lighter. **Size** Shoulder height 1.4m; mass 550–700kg.

Habitat The buffalo prefers open woodland savanna and needs a plentiful supply of grass, shade and water. **Habits** Gregarious; occurs in herds of up to several hundred. Most active in the evening, at night and in the morning. **Food** Mainly a grazer, but also browses. **Spoor** The dew claws, which show in soft mud, may not always mark on hard ground. The hind foot is not as elongated as that of the eland (see page 125).

forefoot   hind foot

Gemsbok   *Oryx gazella*

A large antelope bearing conspicuous black markings on the body and face. The upperparts and flanks are a pale fawn-grey; the underparts are white, with a broad, dark-brown band in between. Horns are straight, rapier-like; the female's more slender than the male's. **Size** Shoulder height 1.2m; mass 210–240kg. **Habitat** Open, arid country. **Habits** Gregarious; occurs in herds of up to 12, though solitary males are common. Active during early morning and late afternoon. **Food** Mainly a grazer. **Spoor/Signs** The gemsbok will dig in sand with its front hooves for water, and for succulent roots, rhizomes and bulbs. When defecating, territorial males adopt a characteristic low, crouching posture, which ensures that the faecal pellets lie in a small pile and so retain their odour longer. Before defecating, the animal will paw the ground, transferring secretions from the pedal glands to the earth. Males will also horn vegetation to mark their territory.

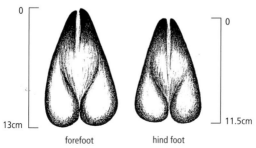

0 ┐   0 ┐

13cm ┘   11.5cm ┘

forefoot   hind foot

Sable Antelope *Hippotragus niger*

A large, handsome species, the old males of which are black and the females a very dark brown; both have white underparts. Both sexes carry horns, which are more slender in females. **Size** Shoulder height 135cm; mass 180–270kg. **Habitat** Savanna woodland. **Habits** Gregarious, occurs in herds of 20–30 individuals. Bulls are often solitary. The animal is at its most active in the early morning and late afternoon. **Food** Mainly a grazer, but will browse in some areas. **Spoor/Signs** Territorial sable males break branches and strip bark with their horns, which may be a way of marking territory.

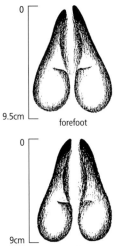

0

9.5cm

forefoot

0

9cm

hind foot

Roan Antelope *Hippotragus equinus*

A large, greyish-brown antelope with a black face, a contrasting white patch around the nose and mouth and a white patch on each cheek. Both sexes carry horns, which are shorter in females. **Size** Shoulder height 110–150cm; mass 220–300kg. **Habitat** Confined to lightly wooded savanna with extensive open areas of medium to tall grasses and available water. **Habits** Gregarious; occurs in small herds of 5–12 individuals, sometimes up to 25. Active from sunrise until mid-morning, and in the late afternoon. **Food** Predominantly a grazer, but also browses. **Spoor/Signs** They will horn bushes, grass and the ground. They also establish their presence by defecating, urinating and scent-marking the area with their pedal glands.

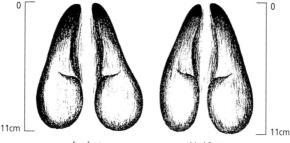

forefoot   hind foot

Bontebok *Damaliscus pygargus dorcas*

A medium-sized antelope with a rich dark-brown body colour and a contrasting white rump patch, underparts and face blaze. The latter runs down between the eyes and, unlike that of the blesbok, is not divided by a transverse brown band. Both sexes carry horns, but the horns of the female are more slender than those of the male. **Size** Shoulder height 90cm; mass 62kg. **Habitat** Natural distribution restricted to one area in the southwestern Cape. **Habits** Gregarious; diurnal, mainly active in the early morning and late afternoon. **Food** Almost exclusively a grazer. **Spoor/Signs** The latrines of the territorial male are scattered around its territory and are generally disregarded by other males. A central latrine is often used as a resting place during the day.

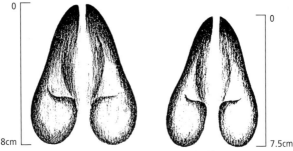

forefoot   hind foot

Blesbok   *Damaliscus pygargus phillipsi*

A brown antelope with white underparts and a white face blaze divided just below the eyes by a narrow brown band. Both sexes carry horns. Unlike the bontebok it does not have a white rump patch. **Size** Shoulder height 95cm; mass 70kg. **Habitat** Grassland, with sources of water. **Habits** Gregarious; diurnal; active in the early morning and late evening. **Food** Mainly a grazer, but will occasionally browse. **Spoor/Signs** When travelling to their feeding or drinking places, and when returning to their night resting sites, blesbok move in long, single files – a routine that creates distinct paths. The species marks its territory by inserting grass stems in its preorbital glands, or by wiping the glands across vegetation (to smear them with secretion). The territorial male leaves dung patches in its territory, and tends to lie on them during resting periods.

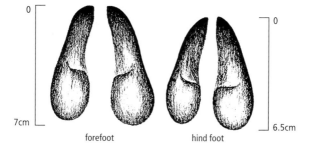

0

7cm

0

6.5cm

forefoot   hind foot

Tsessebe   *Damaliscus lunatus*

A largish antelope with a long, narrow face, shoulders that stand conspicuously higher than the rump, and a dark reddish-brown body with a distinct purplish sheen. Both sexes have horns. **Size** Shoulder height 1.2m; mass 126–140kg. **Habitat** Open savanna woodland close to grassland plains; needs water and shade. **Habits** Gregarious; active mainly in the morning and evening. **Food** Almost exclusively a grazer. **Spoor/Signs** Both sexes mark with their preorbital glands, rub the sides of their faces on the ground, and horn the ground. Territorial males paw and scrape the surface to mark their territories.

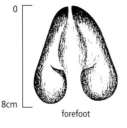

0

8cm

forefoot

0

8cm

hind foot

Red Hartebeest   *Alcelaphus caama*

A medium-sized, high-shouldered animal, generally a reddish brown in colour but this varies according to the race and region and may be yellow-fawn or tawny. Both sexes carry horns, the male's heavier in build than those of the female. **Size** Shoulder height 125cm; mass 120–150kg. **Habitat** Associated with open country. **Habits** Gregarious; at its most active in the early morning and the late afternoon. **Food** Predominantly a grazer. **Spoor** Hoof triangular in shape, similar to that of tsessebe (see opposite page).

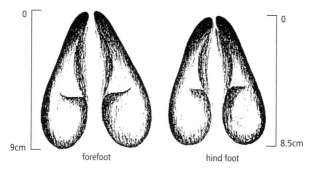

forefoot   hind foot

Black Wildebeest *Connochaetes gnou*

This relative of the antelopes is generally buffy brown in colour and has a characteristic tail with long, white hair reaching to the ground. Both sexes carry horns. **Size** Shoulder height 1.2m; mass 100–180kg. **Habitat** Open plains, grasslands and Karoo country. **Habits** Gregarious; active at dawn, in the early morning and late afternoon, and after sunset. **Food** Predominantly a grazer. **Spoor/Signs** The animal scent-marks its territory with faeces and urine, and with its preorbital and interdigital glands. Territorial males paw the ground vigorously before defecating.

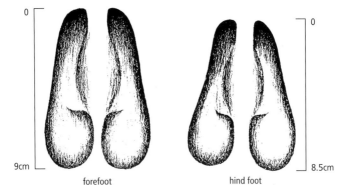

| 0 | | | | 0 |

9cm   8.5cm

forefoot   hind foot

Blue Wildebeest   *Connochaetes taurinus*

Similar in appearance to the black wildebeest (see opposite page) but dark grey in colour and with a mane of long black hair, and long black hair at the end of its tail. Both sexes carry horns; the female's horns are lighter in build than those of the male. **Size** Shoulder height 1.5m; mass 250kg.
Habitat Associated with savanna woodland and open grassland. **Habits** Gregarious; active in the morning and afternoon. **Food** A grazer, preferring short green grass when available. **Spoor/Signs** Territorial males mark their territories by dropping on to their knees and rubbing their preorbital glands on the ground, on bushes and on tree trunks.

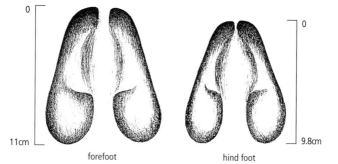

0   0

11cm   9.8cm

forefoot   hind foot

DROPPINGS: A SELECT CHECKLIST

Measurements refer to length

Hare, 1cm

Dassie, 1cm

Small antelope, 1cm

Springhare, 2cm

Medium antelope, 1–2cm

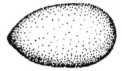

Aardvark, 4cm

Giraffe, 2–3cm

Warthog, 5cm

Porcupine, 5cm

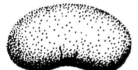

Zebra, 5cm

Baboon, 5–10cm

Monkey, 3–5cm

Small carnivore, 5cm

Otter, 8cm

Hyaena, 5cm

Medium carnivore, 5–10cm

Large carnivore, 10–15cm

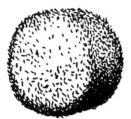
Hippo, 10cm

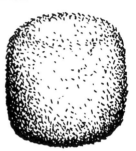
Rhino, 10–15cm

Buffalo, 15cm
(widest part)

Elephant, 15–20cm
(widest part)

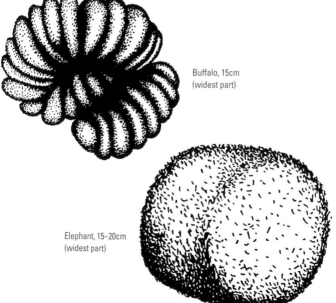

PICTURE CREDITS

All photographs © Louis Liebenberg except for those listed below.

Key: b = bottom, **bl** = bottom left, **br** = bottom right, **l** = left, **r** = right, **t** − top,
tl = top left, **tr** = top right
AS = © stock.adobe.com, **IOA** = Images of Africa, **WC** = via Wikimedia Commons

FURTHER READING

Liebenberg, L. 1990. *A Field Guide to the Animal Tracks of Southern Africa.* David Philip Publishers, Cape Town.

Liebenberg, L. 1990. *The Art of Tracking: The Origin of Science.* David Philip Publishers, Cape Town.

MacLean, G. I. 1993. *Roberts' Birds of Southern Africa.* The Trustees of the John Voelcker Bird Book Fund, Cape Town.

Newman, K. B. 2010. *Newman's Birds of Southern Africa.* Struik Nature, Cape Town.

Stuart, C. and Stuart, M. 2019. *Stuarts' Field Guide to the Tracks & Signs of Southern, Central & East African Wildlife.* Struik Nature, Cape Town.

Stuart, C. and Stuart, M. 2015. *Stuarts' Field Guide to the Mammals of Southern Africa.* Struik Nature, Cape Town.

SCIENTIFIC NAMES INDEX

COMMON NAMES INDEX

GLOSSARY

Arboreal Living in trees.

Carnivore A flesh-eating animal.

Crepuscular Active at twilight and/or just before dawn.

Dew claw The rudimentary first digit on the feet of canids.

Diagnostic A distinctive feature characteristic of a species.

Diurnal Active during the day.

Dorsal Relating to the back or spine.

Gregarious Living in groups (herds, colonies and so forth).

Habitat The environment in which a plant or animal lives in its natural state.

Herbivore An animal that feeds on grasses (a grazer), leaves (a browser) and other vegetable matter.

Insectivore An animal that eats insects.

Interdigital (gland) Located between toes or hooves.

Latrine The place where an animal, or a group of animals, deposits faeces.

Nocturnal Active at night.

Ocelli The simple, light-sensitive eyes of insects and some other invertebrates.

Oestrus The period during which a female mammal is sexually receptive.

Pedal (gland) Located on the foot.

Preorbital (gland) Located in front of the eye-socket.

Protractile Able to be extended or protruded.

Scats Another word for droppings, usually those of certain small mammals.

Spoor The trail of an animal, notably its tracks but also other signs of its passage.

Substrate Underlying layer; the inorganic material on which a plant grows or an animal moves.

Termitaria The nests of a termite colony.

Terrestrial Living at ground level.

Territory A limited area occupied, and defended, by an animal.

Ventral Relating to the front part of the body; towards the belly.

Footprint terms

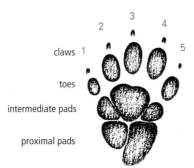

claws

toes

intermediate pads

proximal pads